The Meaning of Life | Hayuta Epstein

Thank you,

To my guides who show me the way.

Thank you very much to my dear family,

Who, in their own way, were my guides and my first pupils

Thank you for standing by me in my spiritual development

I learned from you, how to change and make a change.

With love,
Hayuta

The Meaning of Life
Hayuta Epstein

Copyright © 2018 Hayuta Epstein

All rights reserved; No parts of this book may be reproduced or transmitted in any form or by any means, electronic or mechanical, including photocopying, recording, taping, or by any information retrieval system, without the permission, in writing, of the author.

Contact: hayutaep@gmail.com

ISBN 978-1717095077

THE **MEANING** OF
LIFE

GAME RULES OF THE NEW AGE
CHANNELED KNOWLEDGE

HAYUTA EPSTEIN

Contents

PROLOGUE The meaning of life 11
INTRODUCTION 17

LESSON 1 Communication 29
LESSON 2 The Inner Self 50
LESSON 3 The Relationship Frequency 67
LESSON 4 Family 97
LESSON 5 Success 115
LESSON 6 Abundance 126
LESSON 7 Streaming 136
LESSON 8 Creating Reality 147
LESSON 9 The Frequency of Joy 163
LESSON 10 Implementation and Realization 179

Questions and Answers 193
EPILOGUE 200

"We will call this knowledge the meaning of life.

This is so, that a person would understand that if he can connect to development processes, he can realize his meaning in life.

The more a person realizes himself, the more he will create meaning in his life, and from that meaning he will convey change.

This is done through a comfortable foundation and with high insights, not through emotion.

You need to understand that knowledge may create spiritual development within you since it derives from the understanding, not necessarily from rectifications."

PROLOGUE
THE MEANING OF LIFE

Spirituality was not a real part of my life until I finished my bachelor's degree. I soon realized that my path was not the right one for me. The experiences and episodes of my life led me to understand that I needed to engage with something else, something more compatible with the mind, rather than the matter.

My internal burning prompted me to approach Reiki studies, which arouse my curiosity to learn something different. I have studied reflexology, Bach flowers, aromatherapy, kinesiology as well as many other studies, all related to personal emotional therapies. But these studies did not meet my expectations, and the internal burning continued to resonate within, which led me to spiritual studies, where at last I have felt that I have come home and my spirit had calmed down.

Today, I know that when I made a change in my life and began to study complementary medicine, my true mission had just begun. At first, I did not know what the essence of that mission was. Nor did I know what to do with the field of spiritual studies. Innocently I thought, that these studies would serve me in the same manner that other studies served me - would fill me and make me happy.

As a young married mother of three small children, I had to simultaneously run my house and work. I felt that I was living under a great duress in the effort to lead my family to a sense of wholeness. My life constituted of perpetual running and appeasing. I gave from myself endlessly. I tried to accomplish every task, unassisted, and tried to work and at the same time, transcend spiritually. The burden and the overload disrupted my peace and dominated my life, because the most important thing to my life, which is myself and my spiritual creation, was forgotten.

I took upon myself several roles at the same time. Material roles that are not meaningful to the will and the development of the soul. But at that time, I did not know what is the will of soul, what is the meaning of spiritual development. I did not perceive the essence of channeling nor did I know how to receive knowledge. I admired everyone who had the spark to predict, to connect with his soul, to understand things that are the most important things in the world. I felt a vibration throbbing within me, a vibration that could not manifest itself.

One day I was overcome by a severe dizziness. The whole house spun around me like a shipwreck in a stormy sea. I was neutralized, unable to function. That moment, all the tasks that I had taken upon my life, did not matter at all, for the dizziness made me realize that I was the important one.

The suffering and my incapacity, made me take a hard look internally. I comprehend that inner reflection allows me to have a dialogue with myself, my inner self and my soul, and I discovered that I am receiving answers. This moment created within me the connection to the guides, to channeling and to knowledge, and connected me to my mission.

When I healed, information has begun to descend upon me. Knowledge for various workshops. I realized that in every workshop, the word "Life" was chosen as part of its title, as the name of this book, The Meaning of Life was chosen from the questions and answers stage in channeling.

I comprehend my mission when in one of the lessons of previous information that descended through channeling, the guides reminded Haim, my partisan grandfather, which I am his namesake, Hayuta. My grandfather Haim, fought fiercely to save souls and preserve lives during the Holocaust. Unfortunately, he was murdered when the war ended.

During channeling, the guides created for us, a simultaneous lifesaving process, while my grandfather did so in practice during the Holocaust, and the channeled guides are meant to "save" souls for the New Age. Thus, they have told me: "And you, you have the same belligerent spirit for that knowledge will be understood and established, for the sake of saving souls to carry them from the same old frequency to the frequency of the New Age." This is , my mission, which is carried out through knowledge and books whose function is to establish awareness and connect to change processes.

With the dawn of the New Age, Creation saw a sense of confusion among human beings. relying on the Mayan calendar, that was the only information for that period, the knowledge that new energy was about to enter, had raised fears that the world is about to be destroyed. Many channels were channeled, and the essence of channeling was breaking frameworks and a total chaos.

The knowledge of the Meaning of Life - Game Rules of the New Age has come to defuse fears and create order in the energetic mess. The name was determined by creation through channeling, which decided to descend ten structured lessons that are ten clear rules.

I did not know what would descend at every lesson. I was a medium and let knowledge descend through me. Each lesson was a sequence of marvelous insights that made us, as a group, feel how something in our energetic vessel is changing. The energy that flooded us was different.

We knew that the energy of the New Age, of **Elinus**, was speaking through me, and it was only when the knowledge was completed, we understood the logic of the sequence of the lessons.

The knowledge is presented to you with love, so that you will cross the **seam line** between the ages with ease. (**Seam line** is a period of hundreds of years until the New Energy envelops the universe and becomes part of it) Now we are at the commencement of the New Age, and every insight that is received, cleanses the soul from any rectification it had, so that it has the power and insights to reincarnate from the clean and the correct. This cleansing is directly impacting the physical array that feels simplicity and ease in life processes).

The book The Meaning of Life is a channeled knowledge that connects the reader to the energy of the **element of air**, the energy of the New Age. In its way, the book delivers tools of understanding, enlightenment and development. These deal with consciousness and effect healing processes and discharge previous patterns of behavior.

The spiritual decree of every person says:

"You came to the world to be happy, therefore you have to understand the importance of life. When the soul is happy, it radiates it on your life and your surroundings."

The meaning of life is to recognize the fragile and weak parts of consciousness, to reinforce them, and to understand why they have come to life and how they can be rectified.

When you are ready to begin the process of change, you will feel how you are connecting to insights of hope, to goals and inner happiness, making a small change the beginning of a great rectification.

Creation constantly sends signals to human beings. This book is also a sign. The steps for change do not need to be drastic, but your job is to be open to them.

I thank Creation day by day for sending me knowledge and insights through channeling which helps me as a person, as a therapist and a healer in my life.

I wish that this book will lead you through the right balance, and that you will know how to find your way to happiness and to your goals with simplicity.

With love,
Hayuta

INTRODUCTION

This knowledge has descended to the world to create within you a spiritual development so that you will understand that there are still souls and soul accretion who seek to end the sense of difficulty that is part of their lives.

Many souls have difficulty since your world has created a state of mind of people who are afraid to connect to channeled information that creates change, even though this information comes in order to help souls easily finish their emotional life, so that they can connect to the energy of the New Age with simplicity.

We (the guides) are aware that many people are still afraid of this alteration of the mind, and we want to create within you more insights, with additional knowledge that will speak about mutual understandings of human beings, between a person and his surrounding, between a person and the universe and between a person and the world from which he is derived.

This knowledge may illuminate your life, so that you understand that from the change processes that you are meant to connect to in the wake of the energy of the New Age, you should not be afraid of the change processes because they are meaningless, but they contain the soul need to reinforce you as a person.

This channeled knowledge has insights into a way of thinking and personal spiritual development for everyone. And we want to create within you insights to help you understand the important processes in Creation. For you to understand:

- **Why are there human beings in the universe?**

- **Why does a person's soul cry out to finish the rectifications?**

- **What is the reason that encounters are created between people - how to rectify it?**

- **Why does a person suffer in his life and sometimes he declines significantly to a total crash that creates emotional and physical pain?**

The development of a person and a soul is created with the understanding that a person does not always grasp why he came into the world. The person thinks that he came to be born, to marry, to raise a family, to work and to live the routine life that accompany him as a ritual. A ritual that in time turns into situations of disinterest and sometimes even leads suffering and a sense of survival. A person is not always aware that he has come into the world from a creationary plan of the universe.

The universe sends the person so that he, from his manner, behavior and conducts, from the insights and actions that he takes or creates in his life, will learn how to cope to bring to closure rectifications in every cosmic library in the universe. Particularly, to bring to closure rectifications in the private cosmic library of that person's soul.

The role of the cosmic library in the universe is to arouse insights within the human soul and to send the person out into the world, so that he will live life with the understanding that "the youth will go and play before us." This is indeed a biblical law, but that is how Creation sees the soul's need for the universe: to send humans as actors of Creation, so that through their behavior Creation will learn and draw conclusions for the next reincarnations and the Creation in general.

The knowledge you are about to receive is knowledge of understanding. Your role as actors of Creation is to ask: Why was a man created, why should he go out into the world with the goal of rectifying and why should he rectify if he feels that he is a good and whole person?

But one does not always know whether he is in a good place or not. Sometimes a person says that he is happy, and in fact he means that he is afraid to create a change of something new and unfamiliar.

You know that you came here to a period of change that begun in 2012, which is the dawn of the New Age.

In this period people and souls are connected to processes that result from a sense of control and domination that is barely conveyed, blockages and even energy, to shows you that nothing is functioning properly. It is a feeling that controls a person and causes him to be dominated by darkness processes. The person is not always aware of these feelings and does not always understand why there is difficulty in his life. He does not understand why his life is not benefiting him and why he feels his impediments. However, on the other hand, these feelings give rising to the need to act and create change.

Some of you have received these understandings when you have learned spiritual development, some of you are now exposed, or will be exposed in the future, and when you look at the future of your life, you will realize that you are getting a different meaning.

You need to understand that in Creation, every generation and every age, the souls created difficulties and rectifications, and were lost. You, as souls, have come to life with these insights of difficulty processes, with the need for knowledge and understanding and thirst to change and have a headway. This is to teach yourself and indirectly, you teach others how to behave.

When you come to learn, you become the spearhead of creating insights and change processes that are sometimes like a volcanic eruption of creation. You came to this life because your inquisitive soul sent you, so that you develop and evolve your consciousness. And the more you understand your path, the more you develop your consciousness that precedes everything. It is what leads you to happiness.

Happiness is built from the good relationship between a person and his soul, and this is what we seek to teach you.

The universe created man so that his vessel, the body, would contain the soul. But when the universe created man, it did not create emotion in him. Emotion was created by human beings on their own. Emotion was not created by Creation, the universe or **God**, as you may choose to call it. Emotion is the creation of man alone.

And when a person lives in a layer of difficulty all his life, emotion has become the first place, beyond the vessel, that the soul is meant to contain for its development. The sensitivity of the soul has become very significant. The soul needs to be in first place, beyond the importance of the human body. That is, the human body is the vessel of the soul, through which a person's need for spiritual development is created. This is so, that the person will be aware of every process and activity that he is meant to do in his life through meaning, understanding and a roadmap. These are rectifications.

When a person created emotion in his life, he created the emotion within him because of conventions and class differences.

When Creation created man, it sent him out into the world. Thus, in his own way, the person began to experience wars. From insights of survival and existence.

Out of these, Creation suddenly found itself in a state of misunderstanding. It did not know why the emotion suddenly changed its place, and why the process of spiritual development (which was so important to Creation and constituted the cause of human creation and existence) became second. Thus, through this process, Creation realized that the man changed the order of Creation.

When Creation created the first human being, it did not think that the human would make the rectifications. Over time, it realized that the human disrupted the game rules of the soul because the soul sent the human to live, to experience and create situations. In other words, the intention of Creation was that the human will live through insights of good and purity.

And the human, due to the survival instinct that had created in his life, did not understand what are the game rules that Creation had chosen for him. Thus, out of existence and survival, the human created new game rules, rules that stemmed from new insights that disrupted the game rules that were created for him. This disruption was repeated in practice in every generation, and thus, in all the hundreds and thousands of years, there have been situations of disruptions. Rather than rectify, the human (out of lack of insights and lack of understanding) ruined more and more.

At the base of human existence there is a sense of survival. This creates the existential struggle that begins with struggle for food, struggle for living space, and struggle for life. Thus, from these first processes, the foundations of the ratifications began.

Throughout the generations, the human being's development was due to difficulties, misunderstandings, rectifications and situations of difficulty, but then his awareness was lacking. When awareness is lacking in the process, this is how difficulties are created. This means that the person reaches the junctions, reaches the misunderstandings and reaches places he does not know. He gives up, sensing the fears and misunderstandings that arise within him, and all the energy and forcefulness that were part of his life in his past, disappear.

That is how the person begins his process of survival. Out of difficulties, out of misunderstanding and out of confusion.

And we want from here, from this place, to tell you:

You enter a New Age, you enter transformation and change, and your role, by virtue of being a human and a fruit of Creation, contain within you new insights. Be open to receive and come into the world with the desire to turn over a new page.

And we, the high Creation, want to teach you human beings:

- **How not to make more mistakes.**

- **How to take the insights of your life and convey meaning.**

- **How to apply your life through light processes, from processes of success, meaning and connection from the higher.**

Understand, when you connect to learning and to a process of spiritual development, you show that you are ready to create in your life and in others, the need for change.

And this need is first and foremost, for curious souls who want to listen and change. There are also curious souls that need to wake up at a late and advanced stage. Any process is correct and do not prompt anyone who wants to be delayed.

But the engines of Creation and of the New Age begin to accelerate processes, and when processes begin to be accelerated and begin to flow, every person's role is to jump on the moving train and gallop towards the target.

You have the existential right to be part of the initial process. This is because your soul is a curious soul, and it has the desire to know. And your curious soul wants to go into the world to make you happier.

Within yourself, and in your soul, you know that happiness exists only when you are connected to higher Creation and knowledge. When you are connected to the many high insights that arise from your connection to your guides. As you learn and practice spiritual development, you will understand that every job and every doing that you do in your life, will fill you with a great joy.

Even a work that you think is not right for you and you do not see it as a form of hope, will fill you with great happiness, because you realize that once you are connected to the soul, you ignite within a spark that leads you to a new path and development. And when you feel that new energy will enter you, you will feel that you are essential and self-realizing. Your way will be understood by connecting to a great light, through the understandings of a new way and from new game rules that the guides want to give you and teach you, so that you on along the way, will also teach others.

Understand that the knowledge that we, the guides, want to give you, is extremely important, because there is no person in Creation who is not connected to a process of difficulty. There is no person in Creation who does not want to change his life and there is no one who does not want to understand the meaning of happiness. But there will also be those who think that this knowledge does is not compatible for them at all.

And we tell you: every process that you go through, is right for you because you are in action. When you act, you are in a state of spiritual development. You are not standing still, you are in the process, in the realization and connection to understandings. When you act this way, you take responsibility for your life, you determine and lead the fate of your life and dictate the fate of the way. You are changing the order of the soul. When you let destiny lead you, you become controlled, and that is not the goal.

Only when you act from the path of balance and the enlightened path, you can let fate dictate the path for you.

When you are not balanced, meaning that the darkness and its senses take control of your life and you let fate dictate the path to you, fate can create within you (unfortunately) difficulties - rectifications.

In other words, if a person wants to create processes of change in his life, he is supposed to take responsibility for his life, to connect to learning processes and to high understandings, and from a conscious development, to create the processes of change.

Understand, your life is important to Creation. From this ground of action, you breakthrough. This breakthrough begins from the time that new insights came in, and blockages and difficulties begin to diminish from your life slowly. This way, you will feel a kind of energetic change of excitement, not only in your body and in your soul, but also in Creation. Creation sees the developmental process of your life, which is being executed through understanding of the game's new rules that are supposed to emerge from the correct connection to the understandings and the light of Creation.

These processes begin at this moment.

We want to remind you of Adam and Eve who received their lives from the divine and primal energy that they considered to be a new beginning. But out of lack of knowledge, they created the first disruption of the rectifications for they (as human beings) brought harm. They did not do it on purpose. This was done because they had no understanding of how to behave. Their way in paradise was a road of trial and error, from the first process that Creation sent for them to begin their lives as human beings.

In light of the difficulties you experienced (not only you, but everyone in the universe), we, your guides, want to create in you, new insights that will help you complete all the difficulties and misunderstandings processes that have been created in your life. So that your life and your future will be accompanied by new game rules that you have created, from focused thinking that emanates from the power of thought. Only this way, do you determine your fate and create the new game rules, and this way, you teach others as well as Creation, how to behave in this new era.

New game rules begin when a 'delete' is created in the mind. The cells are erased, the thoughts are erased, and all the stages of difficulty in life are erased, and you and your insightful essence, begin the process as a clean new page, as Creation opens the age from a clean new page.

Understand, a person, in the New Age and in the present age, can change his thought processes by introducing awareness and learning and choosing change processes out of fundamental internal need to processes of change. It is impossible to compel a person to create a change. This process is supposed to come from the inner vibration of a person and for his own growth. You should begin to understand the new game rules, because for you, these are the understandings that create a process.

And we will give you a new rule each time, that will contain insights so that you will know how to instill them, first into your life, and only later in the lives of others. Your role is to receive because acceptance is part of your spiritual decree, which is supposed to illuminate you with a great light.

We created this introduction for you and we want to answer your questions and understand, from your inner curiosity, how to guide you in the great light and to an enlightened development.

Be blessed.

LESSON 1: COMMUNICATION

The essence of human beings stems from being the handiwork of **God**. They are sent to the universe to create, through understanding and thought, the state of mind of the universe and the guides. As you may have understood, you are pawns in **God's** Creation.

Man was created by the universe from earth; from the word *adama* (earth) in Hebrew, the word *adam* (man) was created. From the same understanding, woman, too, was created, for the universe understood that there is a need for dyads in creation. Thus, the universe dictates its own balance, for man was created in the image of **Jehovah**.

We are speaking not of the five thousand years that you may be aware of, but of the many years during which, man has been blessed with high insights of the connection between man and Creation to grow.

Human instinct was formed when human beings, not knowing how to behave, taught themselves to survive like animals in nature. They learned, gained wisdom, developed their survival instinct through observation, exploration by trial and error, and by experiencing situations in which their road was not always easy and convenient. These difficulties, which occurred through the will of universe, are called rectifications.

You know that when the universe wants to understand a path or a development, it sends you, as a human being, to create learning processes. When you connect to the insights and the wisdom of the creative process, the insights of your life teach both, you and the universe, how to act.

Thus, when a generation integrates with a new generation, the new generation learns insights gained through the life experience of the previous generation, just as you create learning for your children at your home. The role of children is to learn from you and from their surroundings, while developing themselves in the process. Your descendants are a generation with a different significance. It has its own growth but some of your improvements are also ingrained. We are speaking not of the entire generation that exists in your world, but of the first generation that began through the process of creation and was the handiwork of Jehovah.

Life began with the first Creation, and from within, the entire universe began to create meaning: "And **God** created heaven and the earth." You know that **God** did not create heaven and the earth only once; He created the universe many times, by collapsing a Creation and building a new Creation, thus, forming 12 Creations. In each Creation, the knowledge was preserved within a cosmic library belonging to that Creation, to understand each Creation's processes of existence.

Each Creation possessed knowledge and insights, in learning and in meaning, that were recorded and gathered over the years into a cosmic library belonging to that Creation. The purpose of each Creation is to begin each age completely anew, with an empty cosmic library, void of understandings of rectifications. This is exactly what is happening in the new Creation that belongs to the New Age, the age into which you are now entering.

Thus, the new Creation sent the first souls with a single goal: to begin to live and to conduct themselves befittingly. That is: "Let the young men now arise and sport the handiwork of Creation before us." In other words, human beings are sent to live their lives while the universe observes their action, learns and records their life processes in the new cosmic library of mankind and the universe.

This way, human beings began war processes that constituted rectifications, wars of misunderstanding and emotional wars. Each such process is recorded in the cosmic library of the universe, so that all insights gained in each age, are contained in the cosmic library. In the past, there was no record in Creation that referred to an array of profit and gain or checks and balances, because people had no insights, and when mankind had no insights there was no need to rectify.

Today it is highly important (especially in this New Age), to gather the knowledge from all the insights that you have created from the 12 Creations, and from the handiwork of the universe and the higher beings, taking only the significant constructive insights, and leaving out the destructive ones. This is because the significant constructive insights have created learning and a meaningful leap for the universe and the entire world.

We want you to understand that in each of the 12 Creations, a different age with different conduct was created. However, this age in which you are living now, was created through turbulence: this was the insight and the will of Creation. The 12 previous Creations created conditions of experimentation, learning, and trial and error, to create conditions for a new world that would exist by arousing consciousness and by other high energy.

This world was created from within the manner of behavior.

This trial and error caused human beings to create within themselves emotional difficulties. Difficulties due to lack of understanding, and difficulties of their actions (that is, rectifications) and the universe was not "happy" about this process.

We ask you to understand that a New Age is a beginning. You are now at the end of the age that belong to the 12th creation., Through it, and by the insights you receive, you will create new game rules upon those not previously recorded. We remind you that the guides in heaven did not understand and did not know how to behave, either. They, too, were in a state of learning, and the handful of guides that were above in heaven when the universe was created millions of years ago, did not understand what their role was in Creation. They did not understand the will of the universe, or how it would act. This handful of guides were responsible for the four elements: **fire, water, air,** and **earth**.

At that time only four guides existed, whose role was to create insights in human beings. Each guide was responsible for a specific element. The four of them were supposed to work concurrently, but since they worked simultaneously—in a new universe and in a cosmic library with empty shelves—they met with difficulties created with each new life that was born. Each one of the guides in heaven had to take responsibility for creating their insights.

As the years passed, it was understood that the four guides entrusted with the four elements, were unable to produce proper interaction among the four elements. All children of the universe began the process of their lives without insights, and were faced with a cruel reality that stemmed from the need to survive. For their survival, they had learned from nature how animals behave. Through this learning, the guides did not know to which element it was appropriate to assign the learning processes and the insights that human beings created. That is, they did not know how to create understanding and meaning out of the four elements, which were divided equally among the guides. In fact, human beings (during the periods of learning how to behave from the nature), changed the array of the four elements, and the **element of water** and the **element of earth** began their existence. In other words, emotion (**water**) and difficulty (**earth**) became the major and most significant elements.

The **element of air**, which is the element responsible for insights, was not connected in human beings. Humans were connected to understandings that stemmed from negative ways, difficulty and lack of significance. These increased the frenzy of the **element of fire**.

Thus, the universe understood early on, that the beings (the guides) cannot not work independently of each other, but should instead, work in parallel through the four elements of **fire, water, air,** and **earth**.

The importance of the four elements was understood from the implication that a human being must be balanced and contain all four elements.

This understanding was determined through many years of experience gathered by the 12 Creations, how to create a new and different process, stems from the transcendence of the New Age through connection to the **element of air,** and the aspiration for balance arises from humans' need to put an end to the difficult realms in their lives. This understanding created a different thought in Creation, that human beings must understand the four elements that are significant to their lives. They must understand that to be balanced for growing, they must connect to the four elements.

Growth may take place through emotion and higher understandings (the **element of water**), through the fire of frenzy and the drive to move ahead rapidly (the **element of fire**), through higher thoughts and insights (the **element of air**), and through a connection to earth and to implementation (the **element of earth**).

This is our significance: to create within you insights and guide you by means of new game rules, how to behave, for a new cosmic library of the New Age is about to open.

The new game rules speak of:

- **How not to hurt any more.**

- **How not to create difficulties.**

- **How not to create lack of understanding.**

We remind you that conditions of lack of understanding arise when the **element of water** dominates. In the first Creation, the **element of water** dominated because some human beings saw that others were observing the behavior of animals and creating a similar state of behavior. Emotion had no significance.

Then the **element of fire** dominated and lead to cruelty that resulted from chaos and bloodshed. But over time, the chaos that arose from the **element of fire** was softened, because the instinct of love began to convey meaning through the **element of water**, and through the instinct derived from low emotion.

The instinct of survival, revenge, and difficulty remained inherent in human beings. This instinct existed for many years, and there are certain countries in which it still controls people's lives. This stems from a survival memory of the principal process that began in ancient creations and must now come to an end.

Hence, you, in your own world, sometimes see countries whose foundations are weakening, whose governments are weakening. This is because their survival instinct (which comes from the first Creation), is giving way to a new growth and rebuilding. It occurs since the world is a creation of the universe.

In every world and in every country, live people who have undergone the survival processes through difficulty, emotion, and development of the human spirit. The development in humans themselves emanates only from connection to high insights and connection to **the element of air**, from connection to the understanding of the end of emotion and moving on to creating a state of high connection.

Thus, there is a deep significance to ending the process of low emotion, and changing the person's state of mind from a stand point of high emotion. This is done when we connect to the **element of air**, to accept high insights from creation, and these will arrive later.

We want to return to the handiwork of the universe. To the handiwork of **God**, **Elinos**, **Kryon**, and all the high guides who jointly created the universe from the first Creation with a high decision to:

- Clarify processes and breathe life into insights.

- Breathe life into the manner and into the development.

- Try to enhance the high Creation through a great light and through a way that is suitable for the development of every human.

However, note that among the animals in nature, the coupling of male and female has significance, too. Males and females are meant to convey the feeling of togetherness, to express shared insights through growth, through connection, and through prolongation of procreation.

Through a creational process, then, the world extends and expands itself.

It is the human being who decided to expand and raise a family. This understanding descended when man chose not to be alone. Human beings understand that it is not good to be alone, that it is not right to go through the world and live with constant struggle for survival.

The universe has sent to human beings the insight, to create wholeness within themselves through a sense of cohesion, with their mate. This understanding stemmed from the need for continuity. For this reason, when you look at mates from a physiological point of view, men and women, in their inner essence, are different.

Creation's instinct and Creation's fruit were born from a meaning and intention to enhance mankind growth, for the sake of enhancing the world and the entire universe. In time, it was understood that the enhancement of the world and the universe was born from a process of insights. That is, if a wrong insight entered a person's life, it progresses and brings in its wake, a violation which, at a later stage, constituted a rectification.

If a positive insight enters a person's life, this insight progresses and creates a meaning that connects the person to light. Thus, through thought and insight ingrained into darkness and light processes, the ambience of the world and of the entire universe is created.

The war of light and darkness began through wrong insights, when human beings were partners in the process of Creation. They acted on wrong insights arising from low emotion. Thus, when darkness took over human instincts, darkness also took over the universe, the function of the world, and especially the human beings, telling them, "You belong to me."

When the process began, the perpetual survival lead to flooded emotion, and Creation understood that a process of existential war between light and darkness began, an existential war over who is stronger. However, the struggle for survival began with an emotional process in the first man, who was also the first to experience the war of light and darkness. This struggle in human beings is termed depression or a depressed mood.

In the age of the first creation, there were not enough people to fill the earth by procreation. The earth was immense, and population was sparse. The human beings lived in constant struggle to survive. They learned from nature how to behave, thus, began cruelty, for cruelty originates in darkness. The darkness caused an essential change of enormous significance in human beings.

The significant darkness also multiplied and spread in the universe. The universe suddenly noticed that darkness had created many forces such as cruelty, bloodthirsty wars, and lack of understanding. The forces of darkness had usurped the forces of the light.

Today, as you have reached the end of an age and in the commencement of the New Age, these are the insights that you are about to receive: to create an enhancement of light to reinforce its position, and to weaken the status of darkness. All the turbulences you experience, originate in a significant process of change—a turbulence for the sake of a new growth. When a new Creation begins, a new universe is created. A beginning of new and significant processes for you and the universe is also created.

Understand this, you are marching toward the 13th Creation. This Creation is meant to take place through a New Age and through reverse meaning. That is, what existed in the previous creations, must begin anew through new game rules of insight, meaning, and light. This is the reason why it is so important for human beings to be "connected to light."

Light must be more powerful than darkness. When light has greater powers than darkness, from its illumination and energy, it radiates insights that arrive from the **element of air**. This element creates within the insights a separation. It creates it in people and souls for whom it is important to create a rectification, for whom it is important to create the change and begin the growth processes through rectification alone, without disruption. We therefore, also create turbulence in the world by various means, as can be seen.

The world, from your point of view, is meant to express growth, which you are meant to build only through a constructive process, without insights of difficulty, through simplicity and higher emotion only. We want to return to the past and explain to you: **How the meaningful path of Adam and Eve was created and how they harmed it**.

Human beings began their life from the first couple, named Adam and Eve. They were the first human beings who were the handiwork of the universe. However, Adam and Eve did not know how to enjoy Creation's radiance and began to harm it, for they had no insights. Thus, they caused human beings to create rectifications. They began the first obstructions processes which led to a state of rectifications in all Creations.

The initial process of falling in love and the desire and the need to know each other, began with Adam and Eve, but it had no communication.

Communication has a great significance in your New Age because communication is a frequency. Adam and Eve, however, did not understand that their lives had to be lived in a shared frequency.

This is the first rule in the meaning of the universe: **to create communication and the right frequency through relationship**. The right communication and the right frequency began to create a growth.

Growth derives from the ability of human beings to enhance themselves, enhance their surroundings, and of mates to enhance one another. However, this ability does not come to a person through the powers of the other, but through a person's own powers; through the knowledge that when I enhance myself, I also enhance others. When I enhance myself, I enhance my mate. Together we create an improvement, through instinct and action, for the sake of insights, to improve the next generation through a relationship, so that they will know how to connect to processes through light alone, without darkness, and through growth.

This is a significant process of Creation because it commits every person who rides in the locomotive that pulls behind the empty train, to grow from within the light. Thus, there is a very important significance to enhance yourself and take care of yourself.

When you, as a person, are happy, you will prevail your happiness to those around you. You will know how to turn others into good people, for you have learned, through your own experience, how to be a good person.

Understand that when you learn and develop in your life, you also teach those around you how to behave. Through your manners, you teach others the insights that were received for you, and you, thereby, teach others the manner and the significance of growth.

When your growth is pursued through a high connection, you will connect yourself to a natural process of streaming abundance, and your path will be connected to light.

We remind you again of these insights.

When Adam and Eve left Garden of Eden, they went out into the world and began the process of their life through trial and error. We want to remind you that at that time, the cosmic library was empty.

The memory of what Adam and Eve harmed, was burned into the consciousness of Creation, and the universe said, "We will not create more humans and give them what is good; we will begin a process of trial and error with human beings." Every trial and error, then, was recorded in heaven, and to this day, they are all recorded in the cosmic library belonging to the human soul.

Hence, out of Creation's need, which arose from trial and error, the souls of human beings began to play their lives before the universe. People began to know each other and each other's manners, creating a condition in which, over time, the man connected to the aggression within him because he connected to the male drive in nature, while the woman connected to the female drive in nature. Reproduction was also done through a process of knowledge of nature, although human nature was formed later when children were born.

The mother created the process of connection to have feelings for her creation (the newborn), because she saw how he grew in her hands, and sometimes that baby did not survive or did not create a meaning of continuity. When the baby was born, the mother noticed that she and the man had turned from a couple into a family.

She had no insights about what the need for a family was, but these insights come to you through the significance of creating a family, through a foundation based on understanding and through the existential need of the New Age, through understanding that a family constitutes a rooted fertile ground for growth, derived from insights of light alone, without darkness. Through insights of high emotion, and not through a process of damaging.

You need to know and understand how to take only the insights of light and implement them in your life.

This Creation process arose from divine processes, which opened the way for the existential drive of human beings.

Human beings who thought that their powers were like the forces of nature, did not always survive. Thus, the woman, the man, or the child, were left alone. Sorrow, loneliness, fear, anxiety, survival in nature—all these began to be a significant part of the human soul. All these established the first stages of emotion.

However, when human beings came into the world, Creation did not think that fear, emotions, longing, and states of difficulty would arise in the human soul. That is why the universe has changed its game rules.

The existence of human beings began as an empty cosmic library. Creation sent humans to live in nature. They lived through existential survival and growth, while Creation, for its part, through its process of observation, recorded the insights that occurred in them. As human beings created a process in their lives and understood their path, nature, for its part, completed the process, that is, completed the rectification.

Sometimes, when souls ascended to the universe, they did not always comprehend that they had inflicted harm. Creation, for its part, was also undergoing learning processes, and through the actions of human beings and souls, understood what had gone wrong, and sent new souls to create insights for rectification. But the new souls did not know how to define the word **rectification**. They could not define the understanding of difficulty, or the path for rectification. And so, due to lack of understanding the way, Creation changed the game rules, and understood that rather than developing the universe, it must take care of the matter of emotion (in both the male and the female) throughout the entire universe. When human beings began procreating, they followed the command of "be fruitful and increase in number; multiply on the earth and increase upon it" the developmental process of human instinct had begun.

It was understood in heaven, that the guides, through insights of cohesion, must create balance, take care of all matters of emotion in which there is difficulty, and take care of insights that arise from emotion. Rectification of the difficulties that arose from emotion, was the significance of existence in the universe, and that is why souls were sent again and again to create rectifications. The need for rectifications recurred in each reincarnation because the **element of water** created meaning without insights.

And here you are, the locomotive of the train. Through your life, you create the **element of air**, and when you connect to the **element of air** in your own way, you will be able to convey the meaning of the **element of air** to others as well.

You must understand that human beings are the handiwork of the universe in aspects of health, creation and meaning, therefore, mankind will never extinct.

Sometimes you believe the world will be destroyed by asteroids or wars. It is not so. The world will not be destroyed because only meanings of growth will be created. There will be souls who will be signified to a short time process and there will be souls who will be signified for insights of actions and development. And there will be souls who will be signified to lead the New Age from of insights, as you do. Through understanding, you create significant change processes.

Extinct souls are souls that are going be reincarnated to prepare themselves for the New Age and the insights they will receive in heaven and in the universe, for growth only. This is the importance of communication. When they reach heaven above, they create the initial communication. If a person received in his life rectifications that indicate lack of communication, those rectifications connect to him and prevent him from connecting to light.

Lack of communication is first and foremost, lack of communication with oneself.

When human beings lack communication with themselves, they must first understand the need to create a state of change, connection, and transcendence—to grow.

As long as human beings are subjected to a lack of communication with themselves, it is difficult for them to be connected to the **element of air**, hence they undergo growing processes without understanding, and connect to lower energy.

Sometimes a soul decides to ascend spiritually and the people around it are not prepared to be part of the process, and struggle fiercely against creating spiritual connection. due to their lack of insight and lack of self-communication. Thus, it creates conditions of chaos and difficulty. This, too, is Creation's way to create turbulences in certain frames.

If human beings have insights, and desire and compassion arises from within, their understanding, through patience and tolerance, connects them to a process of change and growth.

And you, as in nature, become the teachers of your surroundings, because you come from a process of light and growth. You are the nature that was merged from a creational, existential and healing process which connects you to light processes, high insights, knowledge, meaning, and new game rules.

You bring the new game rules to your life and convey them through insights. It is your role to be in enlightened place of life that constitutes connection and growth. Enlightened place that will draw light, meaning and success.

You need to understand that your actions are important to us because when you are connected to the Light of Creation, you become the handiwork of the renewed universe. Through meaningful and blessed light, you change the new game rules. You teach Creation's guides how to be connected to the true light, and you teach them how to route your life through light, action, development, existence, and change.

These insights are significant and important because they incorporate the power of change.

When you teach your souls these processes, you also teach the guides how to behave differently. You teach them how to accompany souls who arrive, through connection to the New Age, and through a process of development rather than of endings and rectifications.

Understand: When a New Age begins, the guides also change. Some of the guides in the universe can descend again as human beings, new souls, emissaries, and as independent souls. They too, can create a connection to Creation through insights of growth.

The ones who have completed their process and became guides, want to experience the energy of the New Age. They did not experience it when they were in the previous age, because they were flooded with emotion. In the New Age that emotion will exist through proper communication, through high self-confidence, through a process of existence, high emotion, and growth. Growth begins through change and intent processes. As you may know, when a person does not want to create a change, he will not create a change in his life.

There is something sad in this process, because Creation is not fond of idle people; Creation does not like people who remain still in one place. Creation supports people who create insights of strength, light, meaning, and power that come from courage.

And that is your way—to act with courage, to act with strength, to act through an internal meaning of light and understand that your existence is the most important in the world.

Be blessed with a process of meaningful growth.

We are happy and proud that you are part of the process.

LESSON 2:
THE INNER SELF

When you observe Creation, you understand the significance and the importance of the way you have developed.

As you know, the soul is the fruit of Creation and you are connected to Creation that sends you on your way to create the meanings of rectifications.

- **What are rectifications?**
- **Why does the soul create rectifications?**
- **Why do human beings choose to connect to these rectifications?**
- **Why is your life accompanied by difficult situations?**
- **How can human beings choose to connect to growth processes?**

When understanding was created in heaven, as we said before: "Let the youths now arise, and play before us," and when the youths (human beings) played out their lives before us, we, the guides, gathered the knowledge without knowing what to do with that knowledge.

When that knowledge ascended to the cosmic library, we began to document all the processes we saw in the conduct of human beings. This is how we came to contain the new existential instinct that we did not know that existed within, namely, the matter of emotion. That is, the subject of emotion became significant in the universe, and slowed down the first game rules that we had sent you.

As the states of emotion and rectifications were recorded in the cosmic library, we suddenly noticed that all the conditions that human beings experience, are in fact similar: power games, ego games, war games—who is stronger? We tried to understand why states of inner chaos were being formed? What is the reason for these situations when the emotion occupied an important place in human life?

And when we created this review from all the souls, we saw that blessed situations, that created a common denominator, are being created. The same common denominator of Creation that observed through general partnership. That is how we understood that all the souls, at all levels that had descended into the world, were creating a certain difficulty.

We, therefore, changed the array of Creation, because suddenly we had seen that Creation did not know how to cope through difficulties. An additional role of the Supreme

Council[1] is to create insights through awareness for the sake of rectifications. But a human soul did not know how to connect to these insights since it perceived that it needs to go out into the world and live, since survival is perpetual. This survival created meanings that the person did not understand and did not know how to cope and how to behave, since he did not accept the game rules.

Thus, parents as well, do not always know how to behave with their children or how to teach them. When a child begins his life through learning, he acts upon what he has access to, meaning, what he receives at home, and what he sees outside. The struggle in life leads him in this road, and thus, over time, frameworks are formed.

However, the frameworks have caused the children to create change and connection to themselves. The frameworks created a vision and conditions of development, through which, conditions of knowledge were created and taught their parents how to behave.

Understand that these frameworks have become a significant part of your life, because they created the process of learning and transformed the person to a mold. Through these frameworks, began a process of perceiving human beings as molds, but that understanding dismissed the insight that each child is different.

---

1   Supreme Council: A group of guides whose job is to try to examine and understand why human beings create difficulty in their lives

When you, as souls, began the first incarnations, there were no frameworks in your life. The earliest souls lived in nature while parental essence was less meaningful. Parents and children were equals, with no difference in status between them. We are not referring to the period in the middle of the Age, but to the beginning of the Age, when survival was prominent. A state of survival means to live and act in all situations with one purpose–to survive.

This purpose in previous life meant to obtain food only. To live to preserve and guard life. There were no understandings at that time.

As the years passed, however, the lack of understandings created emotional difficulties that filled human beings with a sense of emotional strain, and the universe, began to understand that something in the essence of human beings was in need of progress and change.

Creation, through the Supreme Council, began to instill insights in certain people. They realized that wisdom creates understanding and together they connected to the human soul and illuminated new insights in him and paved an easy way to change.

We are not referring to the wisdom that comes from the **element of air**, because in the past there was little wisdom in the **element of air**, and it had no importance for connections such as you must make today.

Understand, you are at the dawn of a New Age and previous generations neutralized their inner self from receiving wisdom. They neutralized the meaning of their desires because they were connected to the **element of earth** and the sense of survival and thought was not always their top priority. The need for thought was a sort of supreme value that belonged to one person, the ruler of the group. All others were his subjects and had to accept his advice and his opinion. He was the sage of the group, and all those who did not connect to understanding and thought, neutralized their inner selves, the instinct that was meant to connect them to themselves, to Creation and to the universe.

The sage of the group was connected to the **element of air**. He was connected to his inner self, and created the self-containment through the four elements: **air, earth, fire**, and **water**.

The sage possessed high self-confidence, significance, understanding, strength, and transcendence, because he felt balanced by all four elements. The sage was considered an emissary, and his soul went through many reincarnations, sometimes as a passive soul and sometimes as an active soul. He was the soul of the emissaries who exist in your world. The role of these emissaries is to create the wisdom of knowledge as a role model, and to enhance others, just as the sage did.

The knowledge that was given was meant to enhance those who had no wisdom. Since their soul was a virgin soul that did not know how to experience, it did not know how to explore and understand what Creation wanted to say to it.

Thus, they began their primary process with the search for meaning. We will focus on them because many people search for meaning. Some of them understand the way they must act, but they also contain a lack of understanding since they always seek a guru to show them the way. You need to comprehend that knowledge is meant to bring meaning, and be a leader for these people. Knowledge can open their soul to a process of change.

Many people have lived their lives with the sense of struggle for survival. They began their lives through learning processes, searching, connecting and trial and error. Each stage in their lives was understood by the soul when their lives ended, whether prematurely or at an advanced age. The experiences that were collected in their lives, ascended to heaven, and were recorded in the private cosmic library of each person. The Supreme Council connected the dots, and saw that a common denominator exists in all the souls and human beings in Creation, namely, emotion, and the job of all the guides and beings is to come and help human beings to be balanced.

When Creation saw that the matter of emotion has a strong significance, it understood that a person must cope and grow through emotion. Creation and the Supreme Council understood that when a person's ability to survive is strengthened, his inner self is also strengthened. And when the inner self is strengthened, the person sees through his soul and understands what are the right choices in his life. Thus, when a person is connected to his inner self, he is connected to his essence, the guides, the way, and to the real reason he has come into the world.

But when a person does not reinforce his inner essence, fear gains control, and the inner self becomes meaningless. The person becomes like a leaf in the wind, and out of difficulties he creates confusion and a lack of insight. He feels that he is lost.

If you look at woman in the past, you will see that she was a very weak creature. In Creation, too, the woman lacked significance. However, when the soul decided to enter a woman's body, she was supposed to feel new insights connecting to her that she hadn't felt in the previous incarnation as a soul of a man. Insights, such as the ability to be feminine, graceful, and maternal. And through an experience of growth, balance, and sensitivities, that every human being needs to create in his life, the emotion became understood to Creation.

It was no accident that Creation sent one incarnation as a man and one incarnation as a woman; it was done because Creation wanted to understand the significance of a human being who connects to this kind of soul or that kind of soul. Creation wanted to understand, through trial and error, and creating meanings within humans, how emotion works in human beings.

As you know, you are the pawns of Creation. When the soul (which alternately encountered a man's body and a woman's body) began to create states of rectifications, over time Creation saw that something within it had changed. Creation noticed that when a human being lives at one time in a man's body and at another in a woman's body, without realizing, he completes the rectifications himself. That is, he connects to the strength within himself.

The woman was considered weak and meaningless in previous incarnations. But when she received the man's body, the man was supposed to create an opposite of that woman. Meaning, be significant, be a leader, stand up for yourself, lead without allowing fear to be significant. Understand the significant reincarnation of being once in a body of a woman and once in a body of a man, because only through this insight, the strengthening and rectifying of the inner self can be done.

Over the years, with life and the sense of survival in life, Creation began to create overload and a little confusion. Creation understood that the woman was becoming stronger and connecting to her masculine side, while the man was not always connecting to his masculine side. Sometimes he chose to connect to the feminine side that existed in him, and Creation suddenly noticed that something in the process had begun to go wrong and new processes were being created. It realized that human beings did not know or understand, what the rectifications they need to make. All at once, toward the end of the age, Creation noticed that homework had not been done properly and a sense of bottleneck started to express itself in various processes in human beings.

Difficulty began to manifest when human beings understood that they were not happy, and were no longer willing to connect to difficulty. Thus, human beings began to search for meaning, while at the same time Creation was sending souls as emissaries which role was to convey knowledge from Creation to raise awareness and establish change processes.

You can see that many emissaries began to rise. A vast amount of knowledge began to descend and many new meanings began to formulate a process which caused many people to discover the channeling instinct that had been latent within them, like gypsies who demonstrated their powers and the visionaries and prophets in the Bible. Thus, in the souls of some people, a spark to create knowledge, was planted. At the same time, people understood that they must search for the right teacher to show them the way. The role of the teacher is to teach people the insights that have been received from Creation, and to strengthen their inner selves.

Today you are at the end of an age and see that there are some young souls who have begun their development process but they have an impairment that creates turbulence in the frameworks. When new souls arrive to the universe, a spark that belongs to the New Age, arises in them, and over time, a gap between a student and a teacher is being formed. Sometimes the student teaches the teacher, that is, the child, despite having a short life experience, is teaching his parents or teachers, how to behave. It happens because the soul of a young child belongs to the New Age and it is free of impeding emotions.

These new souls have reached the world with wisdom and many understandings. In most cases, they come to teach those close to them—parents and teachers, how to behave. However, that does not happen, and children often feel suffocated by the framework or that they are not dwelling in the right framework. They feel that this framework is creating difficulty and lack of understanding.

This feeling is created because the teachers in the educational framework have much lower energetic level than the children. The teachers (or parents), to attract students and create wisdom in them, are supposed to have higher energy level than the children. Wisdom is not taught in schools. Words of wisdom are learned from connection to frequencies and understanding, which provide openness and expansion of consciousness through learning and observation. These create the increasing of frequency in a person to strengthen the inner self.

That is the meaning of life. To increase the frequency of the inner self.

When a person is open to learning, he increases his frequency. As a result, this learning creates a significant expansion in Creation. Children sometimes have a higher energetic level than their parents or their teachers, because they are open to receive, open to see, and are not afraid of trying things; parents and teachers are sometimes rigid because of fear that controls them due to the routine education they at childhood. For the most part, they prefer to stick with what they know, because they either have no knowledge or lack the desire to create a change. Thus, a communication gap is formed, and there begins a lack of understanding and a lack of equality of frequency among human beings.

Parental authority began in previous incarnations, when human beings lived as a group of families, and the human being as a parent, taught his children to live, survive, hunt, and be equal. However, the communal living was lost over the years, because ego and lack of understanding entered, and the classes gap took over.

In time, the inner self regressed, and today when a person wants to connect to his inner self, he must neutralize the difficulties and the rectifications he has created through his life and all the earlier reincarnations, to his present life. Sensations such as emotional strain, blockage, and difficulties, expedite change processes.

With the dawn of the New Age, you must address your children as equals and create boundaries. Your role is to see your children from your inner self and enhance their inner self to create high understandings, not through rectifications, but through growth. That is, to take the child's foundations, enhance his uniqueness, enhance his need for growth and transpire to him that you, as a parent, raise him as equal. When you grow, he grows as well. You need to create within him insights so that he will know how to grow properly in emotional and mental strength, through power and empowerment. This way, you, as his parents, will learn too.

Insights are supposed to be received within the family group, so it is very important to create a family. It is very important to create family growth with understandings of light, understandings of the manner and not of power struggles, lack of understanding and rectifications.

Understand, Creation is tired of creating rectifications in your life. Creation is no longer willing to create rectifications of shared growth through difficulty. These things were appropriate for the age of earth. Today when you are at the dawn of a New Age, you need to understand that a human being is an individual unto himself, and as an individual, he needs to grow himself and thereby help others grow.

Growth occurs with a connection to understanding through thought, through the **element of air** that comes from the third eye, through acknowledging the other's self. Growth does not come in a negative way, through the need to trample, because that way you create rectifications.

You need to understand that life in the New Age is meant to change, the frameworks are meant to change. If a child finds it difficult to be within a framework, perhaps the framework is not suitable for him, he feels that the framework is forcing itself on him.

You need to understand that in the New Age, frameworks will cause a collapse, and human beings must strengthen their inner selves, because a framework that is not right, collapses the inner self. These processes begin in childhood and accompany human beings into adulthood as rectifications.

We do not see how you break the frameworks in the coming years, but later in the New Age, frameworks will not have high importance, because Creation understands that a framework creates difficulty for the child. It understands that it causes neutralization of the inner self, and the child, as an independent being, is not prepared to endure authority because he understands that authority neutralizes his inner self. His soul understands that authority is part of the old age, the age of earth, and authority is a rule that Creation wants to change.

When you learn the process of the New Age, you elevate your soul. Learning and openness connect you to your children through right understanding and respect. Not through differences in status, or through creation of rectifications, because creating rectifications is the way of difficulty, and a person who is connected to difficulty is connected to rectifications.

We want to connect you to the simplicity which will make it possible to create change processes through insights and openness. Understand that simplicity is created when stubbornness is reduced, a stream enters, and openness is assimilated by virtue of thought. Thus, you are streaming with the new souls (children) who have reached the seam line that is the New Age. When you act in this manner, the lack of connection between you and the new souls improves, and you connect to them from the stream because you have the right to understand the process and create change.

All the souls that create difficulty have reached a bottleneck feeling because they do not understand why their surrounding creates in them meaninglessness. When these souls sense the difficulty in their inner selves, it is a spiritual decree that comes from within that requires connection, balance and power. And when that power is evident in a person, his inner self is strengthened by the connection to the spiritual decree, and thus, the connection to the **element of air** is created.[2]

The connection to the **element of air** from high understanding of the New Age, is very important because it connects you to positive thinking, balances the centers of energy in your body, and activates in you thinking that causes change processes in your world. You need to understand that difficulties do not occur by accident; difficulties occur when the balance is impaired in your life, and the inner self is weakened. These things lower your level of energy, and cause you to feel energetically and physically heavy and weak. The moment a person says, "I am ready to listen," however, Creation pours energy of light into him and creates in him insights of listening. This is the stage at which the person

---

2   Which during all these years and past incarnations, there was no understanding and need for the connection process

begins a learning process, and slowly ascends the stairs of spiritual development, through a connection to himself and to us, the guides. This is what we call establishing change processes.

It is highly important to connect to the guides, because connection to the guides expands your consciousness and connects you to your inner self, and a person who is connected to his inner self feels inner happiness. He takes care of himself, he loves himself, and he understands what is good for him and what is not good for him. Thus, the human being prevents himself from making rectifications.

You need to understand that all rectifications in the past arose from difficulty, from being too nice, from being too generous, from lack of understanding, lack of awareness, and many other deficiencies. The meaningful connection to the inner self prevents difficulty. It is highly significant that Creation leads most souls to difficulty's bottleneck, and anyone who feels this, may see that he must board the train of change that will lead him in the right direction, to happiness and to inner strengths through connection to light. It will lead him to happiness and the inner powers of connection. The moment a person understands that he no longer needs difficulties in his life, he will understand that the moment has arrived to create meaning. He will understand that new game rules are beginning.

You should understand the new game rules: when a person creates his life, and meaning in his life.

The person chooses from high understandings and with inner strength, to lead his life forward and to see himself: what is good for him, what is good for his life and what is good for his surroundings. On his way, he realizes that he is at the top of his life's pyramid and that he is a locomotive for his family and those around him. He understands that when he, as an individual, begins the process of spiritual development with himself and his family, he builds a "locomotive with private cars" that can lead others.

This process of spiritual development is significant, because when a person acts in a way that is right for him through connection to himself, he also teaches Creation new game rules. Thus, in parallel, through these learning processes, Creation cleanses out its cosmic library, the shelves of old knowledge, and creates new game rules from the person's new inner self.

And if you have created as a person, as a soul, a process of change that stems from insight and meaning the connection to Creation, you have found the way to lead yourself, your life and the people around you, to the meaning of light and insight - in this way you become the locomotive leading the way.

Remember: it is in your hands to create your fate, in your hands to create your life, in your hands to create meaning through your experiences so far, and you hold the magic wand that guides you to the choice of how to lead your life.

Only you choose whether to remain with the insights of difficulty that belongs to the old age, or to be the first on the dance floor who begins to revel in the feeling of freedom, emotional independence, and inner strength.

We bless you as a soul for your decision, and create in you, from this moment, a connection to the meaning of life.

LESSON 3:
THE RELATIONSHIP FREQUENCY

You already know that it is not good for man to be alone.

When a human being is alone, his soul understands the meaning of relationship through cohesion. When the human soul lives in cohesion and the desire and need for proper relationship—it creates growth. The human soul already chooses its mate in relationship, through processes that were determined in advance by the Supreme Council, and their role is to join every soul for rectification. These joint rectifications begin when a person chooses his/her mate out of the soul's need and the meaning of being together.

Out of cohesion comes growth, but decline can also stem out of cohesion. Various processes arise from cohesion, causing a human being to undergo many upheavals in his life before he achieves growth.

When a human being lives his life alone, without a mate, he lives with a constant search for meaning, through personal development processes and self-knowledge. He searches for a way that will help him connect to inner happiness.

When life brings a human being to a condition of growth, he gradually gets to know himself, his weaknesses, and his insights. Through this process of maturing, he understands what is good for his life and what he wants to receive from life.

When a human being lives in a process of self-knowledge, he recognizes the fact that he is supposed to connect to the meaning of growth. In his awareness, he knows who his mate will be—the soul who will be a mirror for his growth.

But this is not how things were done in the past. At that time love had no significance. Partners were joined together only out of need. There were situations in which human beings created couplehood to protect their status, their honor, or their ego, or out of economic considerations, because economic arrangements were a significant elements that were necessary to survival.

In past incarnations, when one person had money and another person had money, a connection was created for couplehood. Money and property were of greater significance than knowing the person. Class differences determined the course of human lives, and economic status was the major element in joining a couple.

Love had no significance. No one listened to the tempo of love, these processes contained no openness, and the joining of a couple arose from feasibility alone. Only in recent years has the need and the desire, to live through cohesion and love, have been created, because human beings have realized that love has changed its meaning and has become (in the process) connecting and empowering the couple.

Over the years, the souls and human beings have realized that love has great importance in growth processes. However, not everyone has been endowed with love, and sometimes couples remain together because of practical considerations in their relationship as a couple. This condition determines whether there will be a shared growth between mates, or rectifications.

For thousands of years people connected to couplehood through an existential need to survive, with no need for love and no significance of growth. Human beings did not understand how it was possible to grow through life as a couple, because they had learned how to live alone even in couplehood. We are not referring to those few throughout the world who created relationship through love, connection, and growth. It was the energetic request of their souls, to create the connection to love. They were an example to others who did not know how to act and behave. Out of love and the right connection between them, they served as role models to others and constituted the spearhead of the proper couple path.

Today, too, when you look upon your life, there will always be those who are the spearhead, an example of shared and right relationship who will show you the right path.

But we are not talking about them. We are talking about those who have remained in a relationship because of existential fear of staying alone. Those who have brought children into the world, as long as they will not remain alone in the relationship. Because it seemed obvious that children come to a family, and it is not obvious that children come to a family or that specific children will come to a family. This process occurs as a creational plan, made by Creation to determine in advance the needs of each family separately. This is because the family has a role that constitutes a core of growth, and the family has great value that began through previous lives of the distant past—that is, previous incarnations.

We want to take you back in years when couplehood involved force: when a man was strong, he took his mate for a purpose of growth. Love did not dwell in this couplehood. A man took a mate, so as not to be alone, so that she would assume her place as the feminine side—that is, she would be at home, raising the children and taking care of household chores. The man's role was to hunt for food.

Thus, the woman found herself in quite an inferior position in her life and these processes mark the difference in classes when the man was in control. It was he who set the pace, while the woman's job was to forgo her life and her power for the sake of the bond of shared couplehood

However, Creation began to understand that a bond of this kind in which all the burden and excess work fell on the woman's shoulders, while the man lived his life idly, is imbalanced. You can see that this phenomenon still exists today in underdeveloped countries surrounding you. But in the past, the whole world was subjected to this meaning of imbalance between the two sexes.

Over the years Creation saw that it was not right for human beings to live in inequality. It noticed that when the woman took on the choirs of housework, work in the fields, and childbirth, she was, without understanding it, strengthening both the masculine and the feminine sides within her; in fact, situations arose in which the woman no longer needed the man, because she understood, through the inner strength that was created within her, that she could get along on her own, without a man. The man continued to live his life through the significance of being the man, but the feminine power was felt much more strongly. When Creation realized that these processes were not right, new processes were formed that brought about equality for the woman, although the man did not adhere to his new position. He did not like the change processes that were taking place, and thus, began a process of imbalance between the masculine and feminine in the couple.

For many years the woman was inferior in the household, and for many years she had no significance or value. This process had already begun in the time of the prehistoric man. It was he who first created the insights that the man must be a man and the woman must be a woman, but in time things were no longer energetically compatible: neither the frequency, nor the shared significance of the couple, nor the processes meant to create cohesion. And when the man wanted to prevail power in his household, he sometimes felt emasculated when he realized that the roles of the woman had been empowered because she took upon herself all the strength that she could. Thus, the power of the man diminished.

Wars also created change processes in life and it was the men who went to war, while the women were left behind by themselves and connected to the masculine and feminine sides within themselves. They created family processes and couplehood within themselves. Out of lack of choice, the woman reinforced her masculine side, and by virtue of being a mother, also strengthened the feminine side in her life. The children grew and matured with the understanding that because the father was not around, the mother took on both central roles in the family.

When the universe brought all the wars, it brought change. Wars are a creational plan. All that you human beings have experienced as souls, has happened by creational plan, through trial and error of the souls that stemmed from power processes.

The man, who over the years, had come to feel emasculated, began to examine how he could strengthen his masculinity. Thus, wars constitute strength of human masculinity. Wars, ego, lack of significance, and politics. Politics began as a strengthening of the masculine side, to create significance from power and influence processes.

The woman went about her life, busy with building a household, family, children, and livelihood. In her way, she created the significant difficulty from within herself because emotion had an important place in her life. However, when she completed her life as a woman, she experienced herself again as the soul of a man within a new incarnation.

In the new incarnation, however, survival was also so difficult, that the couple did not have the opportunity to create a shared growth of understanding, respect, and proper communication. Feelings of strength and power arose in the woman. She took upon her shoulders most of the world, while the man hardly lent a hand in these significant processes.

We are not speaking of everyone, but of most, and there were always those who did not agree to these processes. However, when the world continues to be run by lack of understanding, lack of communication, and inner anger between partners, this creates inequality of frequency that leads to rectifications, and, as you know, rectifications stem from conditions of lack of understanding, lack of frequency, and lack of communication.

Women continued to live their lives in silence, in decline, in frustration, and with a sense of stagnation, the development of their soul stopped. The fear of remaining alone without a partner and fear of survival, impeded the processes within them.

You may see this in your life, and in the lives of people and families around you, who sometimes live together due to a habit, without meaning and without understanding.

Over time relationships deteriorate, and the habit becomes convenient.

But you must realize that this habit in your life has no meaning. It is similar to the habit you knew in previous life or in years not distant from your years, and it is a soul memory that arouses in you states of fear.

The survival instinct has significance beyond the sense of fear that envelops you, because that same feeling leads you to a state of austerity, which eventually creates rectifications and anger that arise from lack of understanding and lack of communication, and when there are no insights, there are no rectifications.

When there is no love (even self-love) and no understanding of oneself or each other, no change processes are created, and there is no desire or attempt to create proper communication.

Love does not always exist in a relationship, but sometimes good energy becomes part of a relationship between two people who have the wish to live together pleasantly in mutual understanding, so that there is no room for anger. **When there is understanding, there is also growth.**

The energy is the same energy that is created through a matching frequency, thus, the couple's life runs smoothly. Their lives are routed through shared survival for growth, understanding, light, and a shared existence. Life that stem from light and understanding creates shared and right relationship, joining them together through recognition of each other's abilities. People understand that they cannot achieve or obtain everything their hearts desire, and that they must live through shared growth and light.

When you understand the relationship in which you are living, and you are nearing the end of an age, you have come a long way, and some of your souls have become developing souls. Your insights rise to a very high level in the meaning of life because your souls understand that you are not interested in merely surviving through cohesion, like your parents or others around you. Today your souls wish to grow through inner peace, and follow a road that will lead you forward. And you will see the road that will lead you forward only when you increase your frequency energetically and elevate your family along with you. And this is through understanding that when you ascend, you route your life through simplicity.

However, there are families whose relationship is stuck. One of the partners leads ahead, while the other becomes fixed out of fear of creating changes. Thus, a gap is formed between the person who is developing and the other partner. A gap of lack of understanding, lack of patience and tolerance, and lack of communication are formed, which sometimes, as you know, lead to separation or divorce.

Today the sense of struggle for survival in your life does not have the same significance it had in the past, because in the New Age, when the frequency is not right, the frameworks that bound and safeguard different relationships (whether of a relationship or at work) become slack. Therefore, patience and communication have high significance to connect through cohesion.

When patience exists, tolerance is created. When tolerance is created, good communication is created. When good communication is created, love is created, and love is the final stage in the processes from which human beings are meant to grow.

If you look at previous lives, it began with a need to try to understand life. However, over time previous lives continued with the beginning of a process in which each person knew the other and opened his heart at some point to create love. The bond of love began through caring for each other. Even a bond derived from the need to survive but in which there is understanding, can lead to a heartfelt bond—but not always, as we have said.

We want you to understand and recognize the fact that when life is created through communication and proper understanding through shared life, only growth can be created. The couple support one another through understanding and become one, with the goal of shared growth through power and empowerment.

However, when the shared insights in a relationship come to an end and the patience and tolerance are disrupted, we remind you that the frameworks are sometimes liable to crack.

It is highly significant to understand the masterpiece of Creation. To understand that when you build proper communication amongst you, your life are accompanied by generosity and beautiful understandings. This is the right way for you to live, in a right relationship, for it connects you to happiness and feeling of abundance that this kind of happiness projects.

When you are joined together in a right relationship, with patience and tolerance, you create within you shared growth at the beginning of the New Age, because the process of spiritual development arouses within you the strength to create change and growth out of the idle place you were in before.

However, there will also be those who do not have the patience and tolerance to pull the car of shared relationship, and who will want to pull the car of their lives alone. This process is right for them, too, although they need to understand that they must pull the car of their lives with patience and tolerance only for themselves. for they are the locomotive of the train, and when someone wants to jump onto one of the cars (in their own good time), they should not be hastened, because fear is paralyzing.

In the process of your spiritual development, the people surrounding you can remain together with you. If you pay attention, you will see how they look at you in admiration, and see that you have created a change in your life, in your own way. They feel your vibration, but are not yet ready to jump on the train because they are still seized by fear.

If your relationship is important to you, we recommend that you remain in your relationship rather than dissolve it. There will come a time in which your mate will understand that your life and their lives are meant to be shared in the right frequency, which will create equality between you.

We want to state that when there is no tolerance and no patience, you do not create a spiritual development. Spiritual development is understanding the other, creating growth in the other, and understanding that everyone rises and creates change in their own time, at some point in their life.

When a person creates a relationship in his life, people around him understand that a change has taken place in the person's life. They connect to the spark of survival that they remember, in which the woman is supposed to be inferior, even though in this life all those who are creating spiritual development processes are women. When they begin to create spiritual development, they "threaten" the man. The man senses the power of the woman, and feels fear. He emasculates himself and sometimes tries to flee, because he holds within, a soul memory from previous incarnations, in which he, as an emasculated man, felt the need to flee from his home to discover interest in his life. Sometimes, through growth that lifts the relationship together, states of broken conventions are created in the relationship—that is, separation. If separation occurs between the mates, it is the choice of the soul, arising from its spiritual development, to determine whether to continue in the shared path.

The soul, through a person's patience and tolerance, connects him to light processes due to the respect he grants for his relationship with his mate and his family. When the relationship with the mate and family grow out of cohesion, through the meaning of life, patience and tolerance—the relationship and the family are built through light and development.

The human being as an individual has great importance for the change processes. He determines how his life will look. Because while **there is something easy about breaking a framework - there is something difficult about building a framework.**

The human being begins his life with self-knowledge processes. Sometimes he tries to recall what he sought in a mate in terms of characteristics he thought would be suitable for shared relationship. This thought has a great importance and constitutes an energetic summon.

Try to test in your thoughts what kind of a relationship you wanted to bring to your life. There is no one who has not made a "shopping list" of characteristics he seeks in a mate, and an energetic request for the mate with whom he wants to live his life.

The memory of this energetic summon has very high significance in understanding the existing relationship. When a person realizes that the attributes of his present mate are the attributes he summoned at the beginning of the relationship, he will feel that his expectations of the relationship have been met.

Over the years, relationships sometimes become fixed. The sense that "I deserve more" is always misleading. If you choose to remain in the existing relationship, try to recall if the new attributes you want your relationship to have, were on the energetic request list made at the beginning of the relationship. The moment you understand that the list was filled to your satisfaction and that your requests have been met, you will feel a considerable emotional relief. From your viewpoint, the process of growth is beginning.

When the energetic summon is created in thought, a vibration that derives from the soul is also created. This vibration, radiating from the soul, signals and shows you how to choose the person with whom you can grow and evolve.

A human being who lives his life without understandings and with difficulty that stems from a failing relationship, does not always understand that his soul chose a mate for him for growth and rectifications. When light processes and insights join in spiritual development, they hasten the way and produce a change in thinking and understanding, thus, creating rectification.

When a person understands that through his current relationship he can create rectifications and even succeed, he will understand that through a change in thinking and a change in his approach to life, he will create spiritual development. Thus, he will eventually understand that he has saved his relationship and even his family, from creating further rectifications, for only in a right relationship, does growth exist.

Understand, the Supreme Council sat in heaven and examined whom the person should marry and establish a relationship, and who are the children that will come to this person. As you know, when children come to a couple, the relationship becomes a family and often they do not want to break up the relationship for the sake of the children. Children often create the bond between mates. They also create the bond to grow, for through children a human being understands the mirrors of his life, because the children, through their behavior, reflect the behavior of the parents for rectifications.

In the way of developmental life, a person can understand what possibilities exist in his life. He also understands what he wants or is willing to give up. This is a very important stage in the process of spiritual development because he comes to life out of openness and a desire to change, not out of difficulty and resistance. When a person puts aside difficulty and rectifications, he connects to the true essence of his life. He suddenly understands the meaning of simplicity that enters his life.

He notices that his thinking transforms to a balanced thinking, and in the process of an orderly thought, he tries to understand what is truly important, why it is important, whether love is important, and whether the framework is important or whether children and family are important. The thoughts that arise, connect with the personal answers of every human being, and each chooses the way that is right for him.

Sometimes feelings of fear and suffering, which were part of a person's nature, gain control and the heart closes. Sometimes a person feels a sort of submission to the process of suffering, connects to the sense of deterioration, and yields to the lack of energy and defeat. All these feelings are a sign of the process of change that is supposed to take place—the choice is his alone.

If a person understands that he must bring spiritual development processes into his family life, he can change the negative frequency to a positive frequency through a sense of hope and a broad base of growth and significance.

However, if a person chooses to separate from the relationship, he will begin his life anew with a new framework and new difficulty, and sometimes he will realize that he has run away from coping. We remind you that coping is also a rectification.

We are not speaking of all couples, but of some.

In Creation, we do not think that processes are meant to take place by breaking up relationships, instead, we encourage creating shared growth and streaming together through the family. This is the agreement between the souls who join for learning. Sometimes in a relationship, through a Creation plan, an encounter is created between a mature soul and a young soul, **and if there is a separation, there will be no learning.**

It is highly important to create a state of learning, growth, and development. Therefore, patience and tolerance are significant in the process.

You need to understand that your children serve as mirrors for you. Through them **you** grow, through them **you** learn and open your eyes, and through them **you** rectify. Children as your reflection and mirrors, are telling you: "Change frequency."

Your role is indeed to try and change your approach to life which will be less strict and better understood. Try to understand that the way you were brought up, is not always compatible with the way you want to raise your children. Try to understand that their ways are different from yours. And when you see your children in their life stages, and sometimes they resist you as parents, understand: it is **only** because their frequency is different from your frequency.

But if you create the change through openness and spiritual development, you will learn how to create the right bond with your children, because the children constitute a change in frequency.

Children who resist you, crave a parent who will speak to them as equals, will be strong, will set boundaries, and will know how to support, love, listen, accommodate, and understand them.

Understand that it is important for us to focus on insights of the importance of relationships in the New Age, since relationships in the New Age have new game rules. To us in Creation, it is important that you understand that when you descend to your life here and now, you begin your life as new souls. We therefore lovingly recommend that you:

- **Live in a relationship that is embracing, with goals of shared growth.**
- **Live in a relationship through understandings, without the need for rectifications.**
- **Live in a relationship with love and good communication.**

When you create good communication and speak with one another, you are also expanding the throat chakra, for through it you are expressing your desires.

When your insights descend from heaven, they pass through the throat chakra and open your heart and emotions (solar plexus). When the understanding is created between the expression (throat chakra) and emotion (heart), the energy centers in the two lower chakras (the root chakra – red, and through the sacral chakras - orange), which constitute the human being's survival instinct, and connected to power and to life.

And when power exists, sexuality breaks through barriers. Through desire, all the energy centers work through cohesion, with the proper desire to share creation of birth. And this is with the supreme energetic goal of giving birth to children who will grow up through insights of equality, without rectifications, with the understanding of the proper way.

When a person meets another person, he knows that through him he will grow. This is also a mirror. This energy can be felt through vibration. We remind you once again: when a human being arrives in the world, he is the handiwork of Creation, whose job is to show him the way. The human being's role is to be open, to understand the signs of Creation, and to be attentive to the vibrations that are transmitted for him. Creation, as you may have understood, has had enough of understanding how many rectifications a person needs, **because rectifications are nothing but a lack of communication and a lack of understanding**.

And when communication is right, the throat chakra will expand. Creational light will enter through this energetic center, power will connect to the soul of the human being, and love will connect to his life. Love will come through cooperation, understanding and change, love will come when a consideration is created within the person and for one another, love will come when there is a dialogue and a proper communication.

The relationships of the New Age must exist through equality only, without power games and struggles.

A relationship must work through the understanding that when a man meets a woman, he feels her vibration. Her vibration does not necessarily transmit a love drive, an excitement drive, or a sex drive; rather, her vibration and his vibration create the bond.

The bond is created when a synchronization of the energetic array of the male and the female (or between couple of the same sex) is felt to create connection through cohesion. The energy centers magnetize and that creates the initial vibration. Love does not exist yet, but the frequency exists. The frequency has an important significance for connection, and when the frequency is right, love begins to evolve.

The frequency of the golden triangle (the throat, heart, and solar plexus chakras) begins to create electrical pulses of falling in love. And the lower chakras begin to create electrical pulses of sexuality. The communication in the throat chakra establishes a bond through understanding and intuitions that begins at the third eye chakra, which is transmitted to the other mate.

You need to understand that in the New Age, insights will transpire between human beings through mutual and intuitive attentiveness. Human beings will feel each other through inner energetic sensations, and they will understand each other by means of mutual respect and development that will yield light, great love, and connection to meaning.

The frequencies in the New Age will reverberate as new beginnings, like blank new pages. But, as you know, until the blank page reaches the human beings, you must complete additional small, but significant, emotional and understanding rectifications in your life.

Sometimes when people have the same vibration, the feeling will be stable and unchanged. Sometimes boredom with the relationship will prevail, causing quarrels, since through the rectifications, sometimes quarrels are created, although making up is pleasant.

But when the vibration becomes identical through cohesion, and the communication is right, boredom will have no place in your life because boredom is created when emptiness enters and when darkness dominates.

When there is a dialog and tolerance between mates, the children will constitute the bond and the meaning of the shared family development, for children are the fuel of the couple's relationship. Children are the center of shared growth processes.

When the children choose to arrive to couples as souls to build a family, they prevent the couple from becoming bored with one another. They create family growth processes and connect the couple to creation and shared development processes. A correct awareness through understanding implies that human instincts in the New Age must contain respect for people and defend their will.

When you are here, as souls, learning and understanding the insights of the new knowledge called **The Meaning of Life**, and when you connect to processes through understanding to end the rectifications and focus on growth, your spiritual path is also helping your soul in the next stage of incarnation in which, you will be the spearhead of insights and vast knowledge.

However, it doesn't matter now what will happen in the next incarnation. Your life here is important, and when you read and internalize the knowledge that is given to you through the insights of this book (since our words are a frequency), you will understand that you may still change your fate, for a change is made in your life here.

When you learn and understand the meaning of your spiritual development, and understand that you cannot change the other, you understand that you can change only yourself. Your job is to follow your path consistently, and not forget to pay attention to the changes taking place in you.

Those around you also sense that you have been going through a change, and that you are becoming a living example of a successful process. If you pay attention, you will see that others, too, will create a change and will be consistent in their way.

They will see that you believe, wholeheartedly, in what you are doing, they will see your development and the change you bring to your life, and they will understand through a firm belief, that they, too, need to connect to growth processes and learning.

In the **seam line**, where there is no patience nor tolerance, sometimes a relationship can break. If there is a framework that does not suit you and you do not have the patience and tolerance to maintain it—it is liable to crack.

In the learning processes, your insights are connected to the New Age, and you as souls chose to be here to implement these understandings to development processes. We therefore ask that you be patient and tolerant. Your role to learn and to teach others.

When you create change processes in your life, you must see the future and preserve what you have. Because, as you know, it is not good for a man to live alone. And when you are in growing processes, not everyone knows whether a new relationship waits for him at the door. Indeed, a new relationship does not wait for everyone.

And when you encounter a new relationship, do not forget that sometimes you are meant to create new rectifications. Sometimes you are supposed to "walk on eggshells," to come down from your higher level and refrain from emasculating others. Sometimes you will appease the other, for you also have an urge that is sometimes translated to desire and the need to receive love. In a new relationship, you cannot always do what your heart desires.

In an existing relationship, however, you need to know that you can evolve and grow and create states of transcendence and realization. You should not stay in repression processes—they are not compatible with your new path.

You must remember one thing: you came into the world not to please others, but to please yourself. And if your soul chose to be alone, without a relationship, that is a soul's choice. If your soul chose to create growth unaccompanied, it is also a meaningful process in your life. However, if you live through shared growth with yourself, you will have created in yourself happiness.

Happiness contains light, growth, and meaning processes. Through happiness, human beings connect with themselves and with their surroundings.

A person alone chooses the face of happiness in his life. Your happiness as a human being is not measured by whether you are happy in your home or in your surroundings, because no matter where you are, you can grow. If you do not have patience and tolerance, we, as your guides, set you free immediately and by growth processes, we break through the defensive walls you have created within yourself. The decision is yours alone and you are the only one who can make it happen.

But remember: in this life, when you are aware of the processes that create change, and you allow yourself to be in a process of change, you connect to happiness and streaming that teaches your soul how to act in your next incarnation as well. And if today you did not create a rectification in a relationship because you did not have the patience, your soul will find the realization of a relationship through the correct vibration and through processes that will belong to the next incarnation. These will express themselves again for rectifications and shared growth processes.

The **seam line** is stretches across many years and sometimes even across many incarnations. When a soul learns how to grow, it will also know how to teach itself and how to teach growth processes to other souls in other incarnations. Hence, it is very important for you to teach yourself development and change processes to be able to act appropriately for the coming generations of your soul.

In your growth processes, you need to internalize and remember that patience and tolerance have a great importance in your world. If you have patience and it is important for you to be in a relationship, the relationship will remain with you forever. And if the relationship is meant to break apart, you will understand on your own that you have completed a process. That is, you are through being the teacher of those who do not want to learn.

To all the young people among you whose souls wish to learn and develop:

- Understand the importance of growth processes in your life.
- Feel the vibration linked to processes of falling in love and love—this is the connection that will lead you to growth as a couple.
- Feel the insights of the connection to the vibration and what they are relaying to you.

If you are in a relationship, it is not important what is the "mileage" on that relationship. Dialog, communication, insights, and connection—these are the important things in your relationship because they constitute your need for growth and connect you to happiness. Thus, from the desire to be together, you expand your throat chakra and let in light and hope. You open to each other.

And when light and hope enter, you will feel that your life have become better. You will feel that the streaming in your relationship with your mate and with yourself, is becoming more significant.

You must understand just one thing: to be in a relationship is a choice, but to be in a relationship with yourself—this is the most important gift you can give yourself.

Never forget that you must not give up your relationship with yourself, because this relationship brings to your life understandings and insights of great happiness that come through light and through the soul's need for spiritual development.

Remember an important detail in your world: in every person, there is a masculine side and a feminine side. When a person knows how to balance between these two sides, he grows, connects to an abundance of understandings, both for himself and for those around him, and brings happiness to his life.

Happiness is the handiwork of Creation and you have come to this world in search for happiness, understanding, and to understand the meaning of happiness. You have come here to embrace insights for your life. You are not meant to live with sadness or lack of meaning. You must understand that when a person lives his life without meaning, he must not remain where he is.

Remember, we are not telling you what to do, because the choice of whether to remain in a relationship is yours alone. But you must know and understand an important thing: evaluate the profit and loss balance sheet of your life and try to understand why you chose to live with your mate in the relationship. When you understand why a bond was created with that person, you will realize that you received him or her only to grow. If you have grown through the tolerance, patience and understandings you have received in the process, you have elevated yourself one stage, created meaning in your life, and brought into your life light, insights, and love.

We therefore ask that in the process of your life, you may never give up being patient and tolerant, because through spiritual development, you create meanings for your life. Not everyone possesses this function of spiritual development, but everyone will learn in his way, how to create it in his life. And if the family is important to you, the insights and the desire to be together will bring you new processes through a change in your line of thinking.

When there are growth processes in life, there are shared experiences, connection, understanding, and a desire to be together. This way, the growth processes begins and you, at each stage of your life, can create them. Creating growth is in your hands, because a relationship without shared experiences, has no growth. A relationship without shared insights does not create a connection.

You need to know that at each stage of your life you must be engaged in constant action, must understand the fashion of your activity, and above all: do not lose energy on lack of meaning. Therefore, establish good communication through understanding your road and the things that are truly important to you. Ask yourself whether a relationship is important to you, or whether you want to give it up. Answer yourself through logic alone and not through emotion.

If you decide to give up your present relationship, it is possible that a new relationship waits for you. However, there will be times when a new relationship will not emerge.

In the New Age, it is very important to understand the vibration of the energy that radiates from you and others, because through this energy you create growth processes. Here, through your relationship, when your vibration changes, you become the spiritual teachers of your relationship and family. This will only happen if you choose the process out of will.

Remember: you are important to us in Creation and our role is only to advise. When you overcome rectifications, and connect to happiness, you will feel that you have leapt forward and followed your spiritual decree.

The meaning of a relationship is to jointly create a shared growth process, while each person is an individual in his own right. Every human being carries understanding of development, although if a person develops and creates change from cohesion, this process improves and strengthen the bond between the mates.

A relationship through cohesion is similar to a tree trunk, and each mate is a branch. Their shared activity is the joints of the larger branches with the leaves and smaller branches. Imagine that your children are the leaves, and the smaller branches connect them to you and create your family. Through them you unify the family tree that will grow as a single unit.

It is very important to maintain the right vibration for yourself. Therefore, talk to each other as equals. If you will learn how to do this with your children as well, you will sense a meaningful acceptance that has been created in your life which will bring change, development, and great happiness.

Happiness is significant in the New Age, and the right vibration is created through shared growth. When love is in situ, the connection through cohesion, creates shared growth, for the bond becomes a force that comes from high emotion without rectifications.

This is the meaning of a relationship in the New Age:

- **To understand the vibration that exists between you and your mate to prevent difficulties in the future.**
- **To understand how the connection between the couple is meant to be carried out, to connect to simplicity and cohesion.**
- **Most important is to understand the shared way for growth.**

When we speak of vibration, you need to understand that sometimes a person does not experience the vibration, and sometimes a person makes compromises in his relationship. Try to discover your mate's character, try to get to know them again in depth. This way you will rediscover the vibration through proper communication and your desire to be together.

Accompany this process with patience and tolerance, because through these characteristics you create the cohesion and renewed love which will lead you to development and change.

LESSON 4
FAMILY

You understand that your path is meant to be a path of transcendence and cohesion.

"Cohesion" means family, friends, creation—all that is done for the sake of shared growth. When we spoke of relationship in the previous lesson, we implied that a human being should not be alone. A person wants to live together and build a family. Family is the most significant foundation of growth that stem from development.

When a human being develops and rises higher, he energetically loses his roots, the **element of earth**. The role of the family is to create in him insights of rootedness and to connect him to the **element of earth**. If you want to create growth processes and ascension in your life, you must therefore understand Creation's state of mind and the array of heaven. This you may receive through insights by the **element of air**.

As you grow from the **element of air**, you reinforce your rootedness that you have received as a child, the rootedness of your parents as children and roots connect you to your children. But children are, as we have said, a product of a choice. Not everyone will need children, and not everyone will need the meanings children bring with them. However, a person who wants to feel self-confidence and inner confidence (i.e. rootedness) is supposed to connect to the **element of earth** that will strengthen him and connect him to the sense of security.

The emotion that comes from the **element of water** enters human life. Life with emotion leads to the choices the person makes for himself, for his life and for his family. The emotion is not always positive, and sometimes this need inflames itself through the motivation that comes from the **element of fire**—that is anger, difficulty, or even a feeling of control and being subjugated. The need to do for someone or care about something.

When a person feels that he wants to develop and be connected to the meanings of his life, he should incorporate all four elements. The four elements characterize the human soul and constitute his growth processes.

We will create in you understanding and explain the growth processes in human beings.

The first moment that a human being chooses his parents and the human surrounding in which he wants to live, is created when as a soul, he meets the Supreme Council in heaven and takes upon himself, as a spiritual signature, the rectifications and all the conditions according to which he must live when he becomes embodied. It is a task recorded in his spiritual decree and imbedded in his Tree of Sefirot. He receives insights to cope, strengthen and overcome weaknesses that arise throughout his life.

Part of the rectification process is to break through the difficulty and transcend these sensations by will and the need to change. Meaning—rectification.

Hence, even if it is hard for you to understand or accept it, know that you signed for this process as a soul before the Supreme Council in heaven, before you descended to your body. Your role in the framework of these soul tasks, is to break down barriers to connect to simplicity. As soon as you have understood the process, the road to change stems from your soul's desire to lead you to the process.

At this point when a person is about to break the walls and barriers, he must know to stand on his own, and strengthen the way that is compatible to him. He must understand that difficulty is part of life. The difficulty comes so that the person will grow out of it, and understanding is a stage in the road to simplicity.

The soul does not always choose a family that knows how to love, embrace, and strengthen the person's foundation of growth. It is also a choice of the human being and of the soul.

When a person reaches the end of his life cycle, his soul ascends back to heaven and once again comes before the

Supreme Council. The council examines what rectifications the soul has carried out in the course of his most recent life. This is to close old cycles of life.

If there are new confrontations that the soul must carry out, they will be carried with the person as a soul to the next incarnation and constitute as new rectifications for the soul that will receive a new body.

When a person has finished his life cycle, his soul prepares itself for a new path that will emerge in the next incarnation. When the soul ascends to heaven, it confers with the Supreme Council, and there they try to find its parents, family and the life it will have in the next incarnation. That is done for rectifications that would constitute a significant headway in its future life.

Difficulties sometimes shorten a life because the soul that oversees human beings, observes everything and understands the way human behave. It understands what a person needs to do and creates conditions in his life so that he can act properly and rectify.

As you become the pawns of Creation, the whole universe becomes Creation's pawn and thus, under Creation's observation, you create the game rules that are recorded in a new cosmic library.

Creation looks and sees the manner of behavior and conduct of human beings, and it directs the life of man following the spiritual signature that he signed before the Supreme

Council even when he was a soul in heaven. Through the processes that occur in human life, through his soul, he is supposed to create a change, headway and grow. A person should understand that difficulty means growth. The process and the road are the means to reach the goal.

When people connect to each other through the insight that it is not good for a human being to be alone, they do so because their survival instinct says: Family. A family is given to those who are meant to be together to emerge from rectifications. But not always when a family yearns for a child it will receive it.

When children are supposed to come to a family, their souls sign it as a soul agreement to be together as a family. They do so in the Supreme Council, with understandings that come from previous incarnations. A couple who wants to have a child, doesn't know what are the rectifications that their child signed as a soul.

The process of creating the encounters between one soul to another soul is a complex process. Sometimes this complex process is delayed and emerge after many years (sometimes after hundreds of years) for the sake of creating that encounter, because sometimes one soul is more developed and the other soul is less developed.

The meaning of a more developed soul and a less developed soul is a creationary plan that says that the encounter between the couple is created to have a joint spiritual development. In other words, parents should develop each other and develop their children, while the children come to develop their parents. These children are born at the wake of the New Age, they are not the way you were when you were a child.

The children of the New Age are high souls, souls who created growth processes, souls that convey meaning. They are souls who know exactly what they want. You yourself was a soul who created control and domination, lack of understanding, and lack of freedom. Sometimes you felt like your wings were clipped.

Not every person received love in childhood, not all of everyone was embraced and received support during childhood. You, as a soul on the threshold of the end of an age, are still connected to difficulty processes. You need to bring your soul to a process of maturity, learning and development that stem from the understanding of the beginning of the age.

This process is constructed by Creation that established in you the connection to conditions of difficulty, from insights of bringing clusters of souls to connect to growth paths. And you already know that growth processes are done only with difficulty.

We are not talking about parents who yearn for children, but about parents whose soul has signed as a spiritual signature, not to have children, to adopt, or to have difficulties in conceiving.

These processes stem from the difficulty the soul experienced in previous incarnations. Perhaps the mother or father belittled their children due to lack of insight, and perhaps children who felt the loneliness and emotional and physical suffering during that period, vowed while that they were unwilling for their children to suffer the same fate. That vow stopped the desire for continued reproduction, making it difficult to have children, for parents who are unaware of the spiritual signature they created in earlier incarnations.

But in your lifetime, you can take advantage of advances in medicine and bypass the rules. With strong will, yearning, imploring and pleading for forgiveness, you can express convey and connect to souls that will come and join you as your children.

The connection with these children should be based on insights. It does not matter what parents or children created in previous incarnations because the connection to simplicity was not part of your life. The children were sometimes in the fields, alone, unattended and without meaning. Sometimes they grew up with insights of emotional difficulties, and lived with a desire to go out into the world with a certain independence. Many parents had no control over the children.

These parents may have created contempt within their child because of the difficulty they felt as parents, and sometimes they told the child to leave home and that they no longer needed him. Sometimes the child felt that there was no interaction between him and his parents and decided to get up and leave. Sometimes you see in developing countries that girls' lives have no value, sometimes they are sold as property. In previous incarnations there were many such occasions.

But when the soul says it has no need for its parents, it creates the same spiritual signature. Thus, spiritual signatures are created in childhood through a process of lack of understanding by children who felt lonely.

Sometimes these souls who felt loneliness as children in previous incarnation, bear infertility as adults. These are sometimes souls who lived difficult life, were misunderstood, and a collective memory that stems from previous incarnations that says: "If I felt lonely as a child, I do not to have children that will feel like that." And so, people do not remember the spiritual signature they created in previous incarnations when they were children.

Creation summons these souls, who signed the spiritual signature, with other souls, so that their signature would be identical, to create the difficulty in raising a family. Therefore, these souls are connected to each other in this life, to create a veil of suffering in bringing children to the world. We are talking about rectifications for the sake of processes that arise from power, for change and headway.

In a world when a family becomes a widespread foundation of growth processes, children connect each parent to his inner child. Children connect their parents to the insights that they could not understand as children. Thus, almost every parent transpires to his children the deprivations he received or experienced in his childhood. If a parent experienced anger from his parents during his childhood, he would also "know" how to pass it on.

Not every parent knows how express love, embrace, or be attentive. How to connect to his inner child is a person's choice. Not as a soul but out of a child's feeling. That is, where he will take the understandings he has nurtured from childhood and how he will make changes in his life—this is a choice of the person alone.

Both children who receive affection from their parents and those who didn't receive affection, have their own spiritual signature. Children are the increasing chain of growth because they have the desire to know and have the will to develop. Children compound spark of curiosity for the path in front of them, and with their curiosity they awaken the inner child in their parent who chooses to rectify his own childhood, which may have created difficulty processes for him.

Your child is a "mutation" of you as parents. A child takes the attributes of his parents and is meant to create meanings within himself to come through. As parents, you sometimes insist on giving your children the same upbringing that you had, because you think that is the best for them.

Sometimes your insights as parents are not always appropriate for the course of the child's life. The parent who wants to pass on the same upbringing he himself had, is inadvertently causing a lack of communication both in the relationship and in raising his children.

When the child senses his parent's lack of energy, and feels that they are not one, he feels an energetic spark of shock, and tries to test who is stronger or weaker and who he can manipulate better for his own purposes.

Your role as parents is to establish authority, not through anger and punishment, but through proper communication and understanding of what will meet the child's needs. Be aware, however, that the child may try to test your weaknesses and discern which of the parents is stronger, which is weaker. This is a process of manipulation intended to allow him to gain the upper hand. The child's role is to transcend above his parents only by means of growth processes, not through negative insights that tell him, "I am stronger than my parents. I don't listen to them and they don't interest me." Such situations exist, and they are not right.

These are difficulties that arise from rectifications. Therefore, the child and his parents are supposed to transcend their emotional states and connect to the frequency of the **element of air**, whose function is to create understandings and change processes. That is, to abandon the **element of water** that speaks of difficulty and emotional understanding. To abandon the **element of fire** that creates anger, and to connect to the **element of air** and to the **element of earth** that speaks of your rootedness as a family, and to try out of high understanding and midline, to understand what the child is going through.

When parents create these insights, and transcend themselves by a frequency, the emotional understandings of low emotion and anger will no longer be in their lives. All the negative emotions will turn themselves into a high emotion, to insights of breakthrough, understandings, meaning and power for growth that stem from the roots of the family. We remind you that you brought to the family, you built and created, the power of understanding for breakthrough and empowerment. That is why you need to take your children and transcend with them. When you are energized, you are enhancing yourself and your children. You create a spiritual development that stems from the right communication. Thus, you turn your life into a life of meaning that emanates from the right connection, from learning, from growth, light, success and meaning processes.

Remember that as souls, you accept your children for the sake of development and growth processes, and therefore, as souls, you need to listen to your children. Children have the wisdom of life that comes to teach you, and therefore you should act by listening to them and not by the stick and carrot approach.

Understand, we are not invalidating you as a parent, we are creating in you a different way of seeing things so that you will understand that you can also learn from your children. As soon as you are open to the process, they, too, will be willing to listen to you, and this is the interaction of the New Age.

When you respect your children, they will respect you in return. **Respect has broad significance for the human soul.** Respect has high significance whose purpose is rectifications, and your role as a parent is to teach your children the process of respect.

Therefore, respect yourself and your significance, your growth processes, your children's wills—then they will know how to respect you in return. When you know how to do that, as a parent you are also strengthening your rootedness as a family, and creating rootedness is an important process.

The energy of the New Age may cause people to grow and connect to the high emotion that leads to proper communication. Proper growth in human beings is created through high insights connected to the **element of air** without difficulties, because difficulty requires rectifications and prevents them from thriving. In the New Age, your soul no longer wants rectifications; it has had enough of them.

You must respect every human being, not as a human being but as a soul. Look at children as souls, look at strangers as souls; respect the soul because you might meet again in the next incarnation. And when you respect each other in this life, you are teaching your soul how to respect. Your soul also remembers the concept of respect, and in the next incarnation it will send you to surroundings of people that create respect, because respect creates growth. Respect is understanding, communication, and meaning. Through respect, your soul grows.

The significance of the end of an age is the end of rectifications, the end of understandings, and the end of all the negative situations in your life—to create the new. You create and you choose the new.

When you create a new meaning in this life, you derive your fate in the New Age as a memory of your behavior from the light and development processes that have been burned in the soul for the next incarnation.

Sometimes in your family there will be slow processes in which insights are lagging far behind you. Please understand, these are the souls who refused to enter the process of development. They think that development means the end of the world; they do not understand or are afraid to understand, that development is a creation of a significant change in life. They think that spiritual development means being a mutation or something that is outside the insights of life.

For a process of spiritual development to be created, there must be willingness, thirst, an understanding that the person wants to choose how his life will look. He must do everything to make his life much better than it is today. This is how a person can understand his family's impedances, and through the understanding that his family is important to him, he needs to do all he can to connect it to light processes.

We discussed relationship processes. When you choose to break the relationship, your life is seared as a trauma within your children. Consequently, they make rectifications that relate to their own relationships and their thinking. The fear of building a family creates a scratch, a scar and a great difficulty that resonates all the time. These fractions are projected on and etched in the consciousness of the soul. However, when you choose to create a state of transcendence, patience and tolerance, you also teach your children how to create patience and tolerance in their lives rather than having a light finger on the trigger. We are not talking about situations of significant violence or the kinds that drive a person to the edge, but states of misunderstanding out of emotion processes.

You need to understand that when your soul creates a process of change and growth through your behavior - you teach yourself to teach others. This way you are connected to the light processes and realize that you are not only saving your souls, but also the souls of your children. You teach children to respect, forgive, to know how to turn over a page, and how to change their course and communicate properly. This is how you create the meanings of a change.

When you change, you are changing your surroundings. Your children look at you with admiration and see the victory processes that have taken place in you. They see their parents trying, fighting and not giving up.

When you act within lack of understanding processes in your relationship, it is transmitted to your children, who will receive the sense of difficulty.

Children see when their parents lack love, understanding, or communication. They see when their parents are living in constant tension, and they feel how their parents' difficulty is projected onto them as well. And from this sense of lack of understanding and from their subconscious, they live in a constant state of survival within their own family cell, and act out this survival. That is, they learn at home how to quarrel, how to argue and how to stand up their ground, but they do not always do it from the bright side of life.

These children make the rectifications they signed on when their souls came into being. And as you know, the soul chooses the parents, and the soul chooses the siblings. Growth processes are also created in the family among the siblings with respect. When parents know how to respect their children, the children know how to respect each other in the family.

When love and respect are transpired between the parents, the children know how to connect to it. But when parents conduct themselves through misgivings and mutual lack of love, the children absorb the energy surrounding them and internalize it.

The significance of the New Age must be through balance and understanding of the four elements: **fire**, **water**, **air**, and **earth**. The parents need to be calibrated (like their children) to frequencies of the New Age and to insights that come from the **element of air**.

They must be connected to insights through high emotion— the **element of water**; be connected to the growth processes of the **element of fire**, and examine how to yield themselves through insights that they must plant in the **element of earth**.

When you work from of the four elements, you, as a family, can direct yourself to the New Age energy and to the current age energy. That is, respect the will of the soul and the will of a person out of compassion and out of meaning. Accept the person as such because you do not know whether you will meet him in the next incarnation.

Today you compound processes that you sometimes experienced from your parents and those around you, all of which have difficulties stemming from the **element of earth**. And you, whose soul seek to ascend, are also supposed to create in your children the patience, and to carry within the glory of your development for their own connection to development. This is so that they will understand processes that merge out of light and power.

Show them your world, the cultural world of connection to the New Age - the education you instill within your children has a great meaning for both of you. Accept your surrounding without the need and will to change it, and in their own way, they will learn to accept, understand and grow. This is how you show them a road derived from growth processes, without states of rectifications, out of high emotional resilience, insights of light and love and connection to abundance.

When you create the significant change in your life, you will feel that you are raising a generation that, together with you, creates transcendence and meaning. A generation that has the best qualities and comes here to teach you growth processes.

You need to be open to the process and the meaning, and understand that when your life is connected to the New Age frequency, your children come to your life to lead you forward, to create growth processes with you. This is your shared soul signature. If you are open as a parent to receive - you will profit.

Understand, spiritual development has great significance in the development of your life. Through it you connect to the path of life. Thus, you connect to light. When you are open and accepting, you create the light. You look at your life through the meaning of growth and understanding, through the meaning of appreciation and through the meaning that you, as a family, do the best for your life.

We wish upon you high insights, created by the meaning of the right choice for your life,

so that you know how to choose your spouse through a shared growth

So that you grow together to share the creation of a family

We wish upon you, that even if you did not choose your spouse as your soul wanted,

you have the power to grow and teach others growth processes.

When you act out of the right, your life begins to change.

We bless you with great love.

LESSON 5
SUCCESS

In the infinite Creation, you are precious to us, and we require that you understand, in your own way, how to guide your growth from within the family unit, and that you know how to collect yourself and your power to bring out in you, the best that can come from connection to Light of Creation. When you create the new game rules and understand the way, you are moving toward the success we have designated for you.

When you take the environmental energy, you have created insights of home, family and self. You are taking a step towards the meaning of the New Age - a significant growth ground for you. Your path is success, and success is meant to come from the abundance connected by Creation. You are, in your soul and in your life, groundbreaking, and you do it when your inner frequency is perfect, balanced and connected to light.

If you look at the old age, it was accompanied with meanings of pain, difficulty, and meanings of agony and rectifications. Your path was not always successful with all these, because the emotions impeded your success. All those who wanted to succeed, sometimes succeeded through their family, and sometimes they trumped their own family to have a life of growth.

Sometimes when one member of the family wanted to succeed, his family was compelled to support him. A person who became completely engrossed with his success, knew how to clear his head of thoughts, feelings, difficulties and negative understandings, and be committed to his success. He knew that if he wanted to return to the family unit, this unit is perfect for him.

However, this kind of family unit did not always last, because in a relationship sometimes one soul wanted to grow, while the other lived in frustration. They did not always have equal frequency. There were family units in which chaos dominated, because one soul was content and happy, while the other was not.

Thus, rectifications began to take effect and sometimes led to shocks. Such processes occurred in the old age, and are liable to occur in the New Age as well when there is no understanding. In most cases, it is the wives who felt frustrated in their relationship, and created the crisis and the need to dismantle the family frame.

When there is no coordination of the frequency, there are no common insights and no shared growth processes, something in the frequency breeches itself. In the age of the earth, women suffered from inferiority, while men expressed their potential and created it out of their own free will. The women played both the role of the mother and the father and raised the children, while the self-fulfilling man brought the bread.

When you are emerging from growth processes, you already understand that growth is supposed to be through sharing. We discussed previously that when two, as a couple, knew how to grow out of shared processes and understandings, their children would grow up with high emotional resilience, and will not dwell in emotional states in their lives.

When the parents show the children a personal role mode of resilience, the children are also connected to the sense of success. They learn from their parents how to live out of a duality to grow. A person creates his growth through survival, i.e. work, economy and industry that yield money. The soul of the partner is supposed to be with him through equality and esteem, since the growth of a person within a relationship is enabled thanks to the family unite that the couple created together. Growth is done by the processes that prompt a person to come home and feel his rootedness. However, if a person comes home and sees that his partner is connected to feelings of inner and emotional difficulty, these will connect him to the low emotion of frustration and disrupt his frequency, and disruption of the frequency causes a sense of chaos in the family, and thus, the marital framework may crack.

A person wants to see himself in advanced and success processes, and sometimes when he wants to move forward, he expedites up his steps to reach his goals quickly. If the couple frequency inhibits, something in the relationship is liable to crack, because the soul who stays at home and care for the family, is not moving at the same pace, and does not always know how to keep the frequency balanced.

Therefore, proper communication is the meaning of the spiritual development that we advocate through the new game rules. That is, you can choose who will stay at home to raise the children. Unlike past processes, when only women bore the burden of raising children, today this could be the men. In the New Age, shared life involves cooperation, consent and understanding that your life within the family unit should be through shared growth. Souls can choose whether to reinforce their masculine side or their feminine side. A woman can reinforce her masculine side and succeed in any field that she chooses— even if it is considered masculine. A man, too, can connect to his feminine side and create the growth processes that are suitable for him and for their shared relationship. When the couple's energy contains an understanding of shared growth through coordinated frequency, something in that process leads the soul to break through and succeed, and that is how support is formed.

Success is created when a person chooses to connect to light processes. From these processes, he chooses to ascend his family to a higher stage. Every person knows what is good for him and what is good for his family, and this is by the soul agreement that every person wishes to bring to his life. Therefore, you must be connected to the right communication without ego games that create difficulties.

You must bring growth processes to your life that arise from light only, with the understanding that your family is a significant growth foundation that may lead you to a better future.

If communication between you is proper and good, you have the right interaction to progress and grow. In proper communication there is strength, success, and inner growth, which come through your desires. These arise from the intuition that exists in your solar plexus chakra. When you are connected to this energetic center, you are connected to intuitions that accompany you to success.

As soon as you feel liberated from rectifications and difficulty, and act through your awareness—success will arrive. It will arrive because communication is taking place in an appropriate manner.

We have been discussing the relationship that is meant to take form in the New Age. But in your life today, in the age of earth, your relationship is not always a success. You do not always have the interaction to connect to happy life through growth.

When you began a relationship that comes from the previous age, the age of earth, this age created meanings of difficulties that in most cases stemmed out of misunderstandings. The meaning is that the woman is inferior and the man has the central role; it is he who brings home the bread and takes care of the family economically, while the woman's role is to look after the children.

In time, the woman felt within her, the implications of inferiority, of being belittled, misunderstood, while the man lived for one significant role - working to bring money. The women, with their sense of difficulty and inferiority, began to search for answers to their feelings and began to connect with spiritual development.

The woman felt that her soul is sad. She felt inside her that she is not understood, that there was pain and anger for the man who goes out early and comes back in later hours, while she carries the whole burden on her shoulders. Thus, the woman's soul (who is supposed to be the main axis of the family at home) began to understand, from the difficulty and lack of understanding, her internal need for the process of change.

The process of change begins when the soul senses that there is a lack of understanding and difficulty, and it seeks to break out of the Sisyphean circle and begins to search for answers. It is a spiritual development. We are talking about a majority of women who feel the difficulty and create spiritual development processes.

This is why we can see that women are the ones who usually make a difference.

A woman who has a difficulty, wants to make a change in her life. Women usually create the process for understandings, and realize that something in their frequency is wrong. In their thought, they want to create the right communication among themselves first, and from the meaning of spiritual development and search, they increase their frequency.

Men are not always willing to accept a woman's success, or to support the meaning of the process the woman is undergoing. A man may be alarmed when his wife earns money and connects to the joy and happiness in her heart. The man may even employ negative thoughts and may even close his wife energetically and try to clip her wings. The woman, when she feels the stifling on one hand, and the spark of independence that has begun in her life, on the other, may begin to understand that she has resumed the power and is not willing to go back to her life as it was in the past.

With this behavior, she reinforces her masculine side and feels balanced. She feels strong, independent, and feminine; she understands that she can earn money and support herself. With this sense of independence, she breaks out of the submission and lack of realization she experienced in the past, and connects to change processes.

If the woman can connect to the meaning of her life through the success and knows how to do it within the family unit, she will understand that it may connect her to the headway processes. She must understand that sometimes ending the marital frame, may lead her to new rectifications.

If on her way she knows how to preserve the family unit, she will become a spiritual teacher and will teach her family how to behave.

However, if the woman loses her patience and tolerance and chooses to divorce, she will connect to the masculine side in her life, which will lead her to any path she chooses, because all the processes chosen by each soul are in the realm of potential. Realizing potentials that are recorded in the spiritual decree, is the choice every person has.

You create your life and you open it to a new consciousness through awareness.

When emotion dominates your world, it deceives you and creates meanings that allow darkness to take over, so your insights become irrational, powerless, and lack understanding. Sometimes when you act on impulse to go out into the world, the processes are barely completed and you think the path to success is short. We cannot define what is the measure of success in every person. Each person chooses his success alone. Success can be small, and can also be a headway and break all boundaries.

But when you listen to these understandings, you expand your vibration, you expand the insights that create meaning in your life. Understanding opens you to a broader world, an ocean of possibilities. However, to reach the goal, you need to expand your frequency.

When a person chooses to leave his family, and go out into the world, he chooses his life, he knows what is good for him, and he does so through perfect connection, perfect light, with high insights and by walking in the right and enlightened way. The role of this knowledge is to expand your consciousness and broaden your understanding. When a person goes out into the world with determination and insight, he connects to abundance frequencies. These connect him to an ability to encompass oceans of insight, knowledge, and success.

Imagine those successes that are connected to you as threads or axes of light, that reach you when you choose your process of success.

You are only supposed to understand the path to the nexus of abundance that is supposed to be connected to you from the midline that creates balance, and the midline comes from the high thought that is connected to light frequencies from the **element of air**, and moves from the midline to the **element of earth** for realization.

When you understand that you are not letting your feelings (the **element of water**) and your anger (the **element of fire**) to lead you, your path may be the right path. You will feel that you are making your life out of what is good for you.

Understand, there is a high meaning to the current knowledge of the meaning of life, since this knowledge contains an insight that says you do not have to detach and break frames. Through understanding, you can create your life, and bring them to the level of high and perfect understanding, which emanates from the midline that comes from the **element of air** to the **element of earth**. Remember that in your way, you teach others how to grow.

The tranquility that was planted within you, the inner power that creates meaning and insight in you, are what guide you forward. It is very important to be connected to the midline, because that is how you know exactly what is good for your life and what is good for your creation. From the masculine side and the feminine side that exist in your life, you create an aspect of balance through breaking out.

Within your family unit, you have the choice to act upon what is right for you and what is not.

The choice is yours, you must know that when you choose your way of life, you can also break the family unit processes if they interfere with your success, if they oppress you, bound your hands and clip your wings. But pay attention whether the clipping of the wings, the oppressing and anxiety, are not caused by you.

Take a note who is holding you back - you or the others.

If others are impeding the process of your life, you must understand that it is very important to break frames, to increase frequency. **But if you do this to yourself, you must work on your inner self.**

Understand, the meaning of your life is to live through family (because it is not good to be alone) and to live through growth processes, with understanding and connection to the midline without any difficulties. This is the path to change, and in the New Age, the game rules are about to change. The person within the family unit knows how to connect to what is better and not to what is less good. In the New Age, the family unit can also come from same-sex couples, and it is also a family ground for growth. And when a person is good in his life, his success breaks boundaries. He creates in his life because he wants to be happy.

As you expand your vessel, you expand your insights and open your life to the universe – the universe returns your gratitude.

This is the duality that you create with Creation when you connect to understandings through light processes. And when the light processes are woven in you, your success is significant.

You need to see your life not by "here" or "now" or through the near future, but from headway processes as you create the calendar system. Not only a calendar of one year, but a calendar of many years. Take the Maya for instance, how they created their lives. How they created the future and conveyed the meanings of the future. This is what you are supposed to do to your life, therefore:

Treatment

- **See your life taking shape through growth.**

- **See how frequencies of abundance come into being at this moment, and intertwine within you through insights of balance and connection to the center line.**

- **See your future, see your choices and your wishes and how you realize them.**

- **Imagine your life changing before your eyes and fulfilling itself in time.**

When you have finished, keep these insights in mind, and continue to reconstruct your future to realize yourself.

LESSON 6
ABUNDANCE

You open yourself to a new path which is capable to create an energetic expansion of both your consciousness and your vessel – your body – to lead you a greater understanding of the processes. When your consciousness expands, you feel an energetic quantum leap that compounds an inner force that creates insights and transcendence. Meaning, you open yourself to the abundance that Creation wants to give you.

When you work through the frequency of abundance, this frequency connects you to the consciousness of the New Age. It connects you to a world at which you can expand the energy that exists in your bodies, to bring greater potential into your life.

Your life is supposed to be from the total realization of your potential and total realization of the path that brings you the best. When you use your full potential in this life, you can also use potentials that belong to the next age. That is, when the vessel is wide and energetic, you can bring the abundance that belongs to the next incarnation and use it for your life here and now.

When you turn and go forward, you use these abilities, and sometimes you can take from the multitude of possibilities that belong to your next age - to the next incarnation. And use it for life here and now. This means that when you are connected to the abundance frequency that comes from the right, you expand your soul, your vessel, and expand your consciousness as well. That way, you also gain the added value of what your soul wants to bring you in the next incarnation. Your thought creates reality, this way, you are calibrated to a high frequency and expand your vessel - this is the creation of reality.

When we implement for you the frequencies of abundance that have arrived in your life, they must connect to you through a sharpened line of thought, through understanding and clear thinking, and through neutralization of emotions. Thus, you will be connected in a balanced way to the **element of air** and **the element of earth**, to execute and realize the way upon which, you have chosen to focus.

We remind you that the road forward must be routed so that no negative thought distracts you, and you are aware of your consciousness directing you towards the process that says: growth. The meaning of growth is routed in every human being according to his energy, his thinking, and the abilities that exist within him.

When you connect to the insights that are created in your life, you are connecting to a sense of supreme power that yields, creates, expresses, and restores your life. This is formed through a connection to energetic frequencies that expand your consciousness and gradually connect you with the abundance that is arriving in your world. You will not always understand how this happens, but that does not matter. Your job is to know how to accept the small processes that connect to your life, and to be lovingly thankful for the process—because this is the connection to abundance.

These small processes connect human beings to a whole and full life that yields a process that is called happiness, because **the meaning of happiness is growth.**

Happy people have the desire to grow, that is their goal. Their thoughts are devoted to the process of growth, and through this understanding, they expand the energy within them and create spiritual development. This may not always occur through words; in most cases people act through internal awareness and pure desires.

This happens when a creative thought is sent to Creation. Through awareness and understanding, an individual's desires are transmitted to Creation and it does the work for him—this is a reality-creating thought, the significance of which, is expansion and growth.

This should be the aspiration of every human being—to be connected to frequencies of abundance—because they express the sense of happiness in humans. When human beings are aware of happiness, they are always active, they see themselves several steps ahead, do not stagnate, thus, enable the soul to break through limitations of fear.

Understand, your success is important to us. We, your guides, come to your life to prompt you and give you an energetic "push." You may see us as a tailwind that creates a new way for you to produce insights of growth and transcendence through connection to the Light of Creation. Your way is to look ahead through growth.

Note that we sometimes repeat ourselves so that our words can become a mantra for you, a mantra that changes your way of thinking. We do this because we believe in you - you deserve to succeed! you deserve to succeed through the insights that push you forward.

Remember, **you deserve to succeed!** Make these words a mantra:

- **I deserve to succeed!**
- **I deserve to create meaning in my life!**
- **I am deserving!**
- **I am deserving because I have changed my thinking and am ready to realize my life anew.**

You deserve to receive, because you have created proper communication within yourself. You have created a new self in your life, through the right relationship between yourself and your surroundings and growth is the new containment in your life.

By doing so, you have created within yourself a correct and balanced process that we call encompassing, growth, and abundance.

We repeat this again and again and seek to create in you insights that will change the beliefs that have limited you, so that your brain will eliminate the negative thinking that was part of the education you received and will connect you to balanced and enlightened thinking. We are calibrating your line of thinking to be all positive, and to be connected to the energy of light.

Remember, these words are a mantra. Look ahead through the consciousness of abundance, and connect your conscience from midline to the future:

Do not be afraid.
Create new insights and meanings in your life
Look ahead and see the future which you choose to see.
Do it now…

We have connected you to frequencies of abundance because it is important to us that you succeed. You matter a great deal to us, and it is important to us that you understand your way, because until now you did not know that we exist and are prepared to stand at your side. Until now we have not explained our way for you, and have not told you that you are the pillar of your life.

You came here from a creational plan that constructed success only. Out of your life, and from the understandings you have collected in your life, you may choose what meaning to bring to your life. All these constitute a creational plan of happiness.

When you feel that you are connecting to this plan, you will feel an inner peace within that stems from a life of simplicity and stream through insights that have been liberated from the rectifications of your life and are connected to abundance frequencies that bring light and glory to your life.

When you succeed—success means a frequency of abundance.

When you live in happiness and at peace with the members of your household—these are frequencies of abundance.

The frequencies of abundance exist in the universe and there are many, but you cannot always perceive them. Therefore, it is very important to expand your consciousness, so that you illuminate yourself through many frequencies of light and meaning.

We wish upon you:

May you always know to open your eyes to environmental understandings,

May you know to illuminate fullness and meaning,

May you know to create the best and the better,

May you know what is essential and what is unimportant,

May you know how to illuminate understandings in what is unimportant, and implement them for yourself on your way,

May you understand that the meaning of life is all that you aspire to for yourself,

And when you act through positive, pure thought, and through the understandings that you deserve to receive—may you indeed receive.

But remember, Creation has its own pace, and all these are driven by the pace of your growth, through processes that say: let go of the past, set it free and through it, create meaning of growth.

When you do this properly and through what is right, and when you welcome insights, your way will be connected to abundance.

We wish upon you that all your understandings be enlightened, through open doors, without frames, without walls, without defenses, through broad vision with a view to your future, to what is good for you, and what you are meant to do. May you use the abundance in the way that leads to growth.

Look ahead, for this will be your way forever.

CONNECTION TO THE FREQUENCY OF ABUNDANCE—MEDITATION

Close your eyes and take three breaths...

Smile for the future of the world and try to understand that this future lies beneath your feet as a blooming green meadow.

In your life processes everyone is an individual, and all the very high souls seek growth processes.

We wish you wisdom and insight to use these tools for light, to create growth and to convey meaning.

We wish you to take the difficulty, leave it behind you, and know that you are heading towards the New Age to create meaning and growth processes.

Do not look back, do not look at your life with the awareness of soul-searching, it does not matter now.

Imagine you shed the cloak of difficulty from your life and start new beginnings.

Feel how the cloak of difficulty is lying on the floor of the past... Step forward and say goodbye to the cloak of difficulty left on the ground.

Feel how your shoulders create lightness and simplicity. Your soul also connects to simplicity, it connects to the meaning of life.

See how white light is descending from heaven and floods your whole body in a bath of light.

Breathe the energetic light and see yourself as golden, illuminated, and meaningful.

See your body illuminated and breathe the white light... inhale it inside you.

Keep breathing the glory of light until you feel that you are filled with the frequency of the new energy.

And with a creative thought, create the reality of your life... do it now.

And if you are done, see how a new door opens... step in... and see a new world unfolding before you.

A new and bright world, full of energetic conduits of light that want to connect with you.

Go inside, this is your new place.

Feel how new doors open for you and old doors close.

Remember:

When you create a permanent meaning in your life – you are constantly connected to light frequencies. The choice is yours.

Understanding is the inner force that you are supposed to connect to, therefore:

See each decision to create a change, as a new beginning.

LESSON 7
STREAMING

When you created your development from your abundance frequencies, you understood that the road that yield the streams for you, is supposed to be through purity and creative thought. When you live with streaming, your life opens to you as a pool of potentials emanating from high light and connection to Creation for the sake of realization.

When you are at high frequency, you feel a surge of abundance that leads you forward to a way of life that emerges from the connection to the **element of air**. The goal for you is to absorb as much data as possible that wants to connect with you from the Light of Creation, so that a frequency coordination will be established between you and Creation and for you to be open to accept and understand what your spiritual decree wants for you. All these will connect you to spatial vision.

Spatial vision is valuable. It opens your consciousness and connects you to a great light that will stream through you.

If your life is routed by the stream, you are connected to the insights that come from the **element of air**. These develop your intuitions, senses and sensors that awaken the third eye and the solar plexus to a common bond between you and Creation. Your heart opens to Creation that creates meaning in you.

In your special way, you become the Creation's cherished beings and its essence. You become the main and the most important thing for us in Creation because you act differently than you did before.

This is the stream of life and this is the understanding we wish for you to create in your life. This is how you expand your vessel, expand your mind and connect with us even more. Your vessel is connected to high understanding and development that leads you forward. As you walk your way through the drops, you activate your intuitions that merge out of the stream. It is your growth, and it has a significant connection to the stream of life. That is how your path emerges - from simplicity and your connection to light. Clarity is created to realize the goals you set in your life.

Your soul too, becomes happy when you act correctly. On its way, it collects all the fragments that you have lost during the course of your life. Soul fragments of memories in which you did not know how to stand on your own, you felt defeated and created rectifications and emotional pain that remains burned in the memory of your soul. These were torn from your aura, and rose as the soulful memory of the moment of awareness and moment of change.

When your energy lacks the soul fragments, you feel the darkness that becomes part of your life. But when the soul fragments return to your aura, you will feel how the light connects to you in full, and helps you fight the darkness.

This is the role of the streamline between you and Creation - to bring you into the light, to create within you the courage to do, and to show you the way to your spiritual decree. It is the soul's way of bringing happiness to your life.

The soul can enlighten you and connect you to abundance and to the future. You need to do this with the help of spatial vision, that is who you are, improving your relationship with Creation. Thus, your soul expands its vessel and its consciousness. This is the healing process you call 'coincidence' or 'karma'. This process is created when all four elements are connected through balance.

Going between the drops, means, creating a frequency comparison with each other. That is, to listen to the surrounding, to be receptive, and to accept, between the drops, situations that are supposed to serve you in your life and you are meant to convey meaning with them.

Thus, out of the streaming and simplicity that adhere to your life, you also elevate those who interact with you.

It is not good to be alone, and sometimes along the way, you also raise those around you energetically, and create meaning and streaming with them. That way, you become the locomotive, and the others "get aboard" the train with love, willingly and through simplicity.

As a "spiritual teacher", do not forget this, you came to learn and empower yourself first, and then teach others how to behave in the manner of change. This is how you show them the way and you also sweep them to create meaning.

To be connected to the stream, just look at life and see how you drive it for your own good.

Your life here on the **seam line** of the age, has a meaning of difficulty stemming from incomprehension. Sometimes you make life difficult by choice and will. You like this "comfortable" feeling because it comes from a whole life of habits that impede you. That is how difficulty enters. But if you realize that the change processes bring to your life an abundance, in the shape of expanding your consciousness, you will feel that you are becoming the real thing - to lead your mind forward.

It is enough for you to see simple examples from your life, that will slowly develop your consciousness. It is enough for you to see tiny bits of abundance that will be scattered in your life and connect you to the stream. This is how you will develop your consciousness and learn how to "walk between the drops".

When a person lives his life, and walks between the drops, or on the tips of his fingers, all his life, he diminishes himself. He is afraid, he feels dwarfed, he connects to the sense of darkness and creates incomprehension, lack of connection, and unrest in his world.

As you learn and develop, you try to teach the people around you how to create change and walk with them between the drops. Your surroundings do not always understand your way and you are not willing to "offend" them, but your life is redirected differently. They are routed forward out of growth and understanding the meaning of life.

If you expand your vessel, you will no longer need to clip your wings, shrink or fear that you are hurting others. That is not the intention. **You** become the "droplets" (the meaning) that others will fear to get "wet" by, because you have compounded within your life and your soul, a blessed growth.

You, and only you, become important. Your mind should do only what is good for you. But remember, you may not hurt others. You need to act with an inner sense that you are following the right path.

Remember, do not confine yourself anymore. Your job is to develop your consciousness and choose to be the most important person that Creation cherishes.

Chose to be the one, the most significant and special fruit of Creation. Familiarize yourself with your abilities and awareness. That is how you establish spiritual development and expand your vessel.

Choose to connect to "here" and "now" and to abundance. See how you create your life from a connection to the Light of Creation, because your path says: Future.

When you are coping with processes that you have been afraid to cope before, you connect to the sense of courage that builds your future from light.

This way you become the meaning. You become the way. You become the object of admiration for those who have not yet boarded the train, and the ones who have not yet discovered that there is a train station in Creation. And so out of a new consciousness and from the expansion of the vessel, you changed your role. You have become the strongest in your surroundings and created it out of the right frequency and through power and inner strength coming out of your Solar Plexus. This is how you connect to the Light of Creation, that is, to your intuitions. The Light of Creation is a tailwind for you that calibrates your thought to think of a future. This is the streamline.

You do not have to look at your behavior or your breeding, whether it is over-consideration, over-kindness, or over-indulgence. You become the streamline of your life. You become the high tide - the creek that leads to the open sea.

Imagine that the creek has dried because the sun has evaporated the water and the rain has not fallen. The creek became an arroyo, because the water sank into the ground. And when the first rain began, the trickle of water began to fill the arroyo again. Imagine the dripping of the water that starts from a gentle drizzle, turning into a, seemingly meaningless, gentle flow, but it is the first to quench the thirsty soil, the first to create the meaning.

You are like this arroyo. You created meaning when you changed your way and saturated a hard soil (the **element of earth**) that created in your life states of difficulty and incomprehension.

When the hard soil softens a bit, the initial current becomes a full surge of water, happiness, abundance and life.

The creek begins to yield life, suddenly it becomes a strong river, a river that supplies water all year round, and the water that stream into the open sea, to the ocean that creates in your life, brings a variety of possibilities that you will nurture from within you.

You have the right to choose whether to fill a small lake, a sea or an ocean, or to be a drop in the ocean. Remember that a drop in the sea sometimes has meaning. A drop and another drop, become a puddle, and this puddle sometimes quenches your thirst and the thirst of those who need it.

Remember, you are on your way to create meaning, convey the vision of success that creates a future in your life. As the streaming and expansion of the vessel makes sense, your vessel will be wider and more productive. Thus, the flow will be vibrant and fill lakes and oceans that need your water. The oceans are the people, the insights that you are supposed to impart. The water is you.

All these are according to your ability to contain. The ability each person has, to connect and give from within.

The meaning of life is every point that you have created in your life. Any understanding that you connect to and create abundance with, any road that yields your own path, through inner growth and connection to the One, and the connection to One is you. You are significant, and your direction is forward. And as the creek knows where it will flow: To the sea, to the pond, to the lake or to the ocean, you can see your future to route your life with purpose. Understand where you want to get in your life, what do you want to do and how you see yourself at that point in time. Thought creates change and creates the reality of your life.

You can increase the frequency and you can decide to decrease it.

You have the power to create meaning and the power to halt your life and stay put.

Only by doing, you connect to the meaning of life and streaming. When you come up with an idea and do not apply it, you stop the streamline of your life.

The thought that directs you to see the future is what creates your future. The meaning of a thought that sees a future, is to act and not to stay put, to create and to convey meaning, each in his own way and in his own understandings.

Remember:

Doing is not to sit idly by. Sometimes people sit back and wait for Creation to lead them, guide them and work for them - no.

Doing is to take your life and lead it to a meaning through trial and error, and never stop.

If a path is open, you must try and see if it is the right path for you or not. If it is not right, go back and open a new door until you feel that this is the streamline of your life.

Do not give up when you feel failure.

Do not give up when you feel that your life is blocked and that all doors are closed for you.

Do not give up when a door closes, it is just a sign that it was not right for you. And when such a thing happens, there will always be a new door that opens.

Each new door produces a new world, new experiences and new understandings. Sometimes you only need to experience the process and try to open the door, and sometimes you have exhausted the experience from the door that opens, even if the experience is minor.

When you feel that a door is closing, go back to the starting point, to the inner self, to the feeling of the here and now. Try to understand, from the internal connection, and from the intuitions within the Solar Plexus, what goes on inside and what do you need to understand in the process you have experienced.

Keep trying and do not give up. You must not connect to the sense of defeat. Do not let it in at all because defeat is a process of darkness and you must not be connected to darkness.

Your job is to try, and try to go with the flow and understand what is good for your life. You must try constantly and not despair. Not think that you are a loser and feel depressed, dark and give up, no. We do not agree with this state of mind.

We create a new direction within you, which is supposed to lead you to see through light and meaning. Trial and error processes, are of great significance to your life, even from a process of courage. Therefore, you must keep trying to open doors, see what is behind each door and draw your own conclusions. Thus, by connection with your intuitions, ask yourself and wait for answers that will guide you along the way.

The connection to the inner self, to the here and now, constitutes a connection to yourself. It is what is helping you to expand your consciousness and open doors and new ways to your life.

As you expand your vessel and consciousness, you can set new goals before your eyes and act with the highest emotion and high thought alone.

This is the way, not to connect to negative thoughts. Do not connect to difficulties and misunderstandings.

To connect to the meaning of life that is manifested in a manner of streaming.

And when you understand the way, your soul is skyrocketing, happy and confirming your path according to the right.

LESSON 8
CREATING REALITY

On your way in life, as you have been creating the way you have followed until now, you create the reality of your life, through the stream of life—although you do not always do this knowingly.

When you wish to create reality, the way is through the stream of life and the insights you have created in your life.

When you incorporate belief, and stream with your life rather than struggle with it, you are acting through processes that are right for you, and are not wasting your energy on incomprehension and meaning.

Thus, through your aura, when your road is understood, you are calibrated to the midline.

The frequency significance of all the change processes you have undergone so far, should be accompanied by questions you must ask yourself with the goal of growing by envisioning the future:

For the sake of your personal growth process, ask yourself:

- **How do I shape my life and create the reality of my life?**
- **How do I take my life and yield a great light?**
- **How does Creation create the best for me?**
- **How do I connect to processes that create realization and prosperity?**

You need to understand that prosperity means growth for you, by insights that Creation has simplified for you, to understand what success means.

In the process of creating reality, you need to create from the **element of earth** and the **element of air**, whose function is to pull forward.

The **element of air** is connected to the human being's spiritual decree and is controlled by high Creation. It sees all the processes in Creation, and is calibrated with understandings of potential that are recorded in your spiritual decree. Thus, when you want to create a reality, you are supposed to do so according to the limits of your ability and understanding.

Start to create immediate goals, then future goals, and long-term goals. The goals should be logical. Do not be angry at Creation if it does not comply with your desires.

Your way of creating a reality should be from the soul potential that is pre-recorded. The reality of your life needs to come from a right relationship, the summon for a family (for all those who have no family or no relationship), summon a livelihood, summon a success and summon realization.

This is the way you create the first reality that Creation has entrusted to you.

When you seek to create a reality, you strengthen your connection with the guides and Creation, and you help yourself to realize the happiness processes in your life.

The ultimate role of creating a reality, is to connect you to a higher Creation and to create within you a belief that Creation is on your side and cherishes you. This is how you open to Creation and form a contact with it. You accept it in the small signs that Creation sends you and tells you in its own way: I am with you, I protect you and I am connected to you.

When you understand your road, you create nobility, because you understand that there is also a way to create a higher and larger reality that has meanings of connection with the guides. This process is important, and stems from an inner belief and a balanced frequency that is emerging from the four elements. You connect to it with a clear, creative and clean thought that leads you, with the most forceful energetic power, to the goal.

When you create reality, or try to create a reality, you need to create a kind of script, and see how the first stage begins, how the road is conducted and how the result takes shape.

You can see yourself creating a reality with other people, who will help you on the way, or with any means that can make things easier for you in the process. The main thing is that you see the goal.

You can also specify times. Time motivates you and drive you to awareness that you need to finish the process. But understand, time has a meaning only for you, not for Creation.

An important part of the process of creating a reality, is to converge within yourself when you separate the thoughts of futility and the chaos that are created in your life, and separate everything that "contaminates" your frequency. Thus, from self-converge and fine-tuning your thought, you will see yourself realizing it.

To create your own reality, your frequency must be clean, with massive tuning to success and vision.

Do not look at the "here" and "now", see the future only through allocating. Imagine how you see yourself in a month, in a year or in five years. This is the process that you need to build through your life scenario, with no room left for emotion.

In the New Age, emotion negates itself and the creation of reality occupies a significant place. In the New Age, a balanced frequency will be a part of every person's life cycle. Every person will live his life from this frequency while creating the reality of his life.

There will be times when the thought will create the same reality in some people. This is the result of a creational plan that emanates from the Supreme Consciousness and the Supreme Council, which connect the souls to growth and shared creation.

You can see it in relationships, in start-up companies and other fields of life. This is because the world processes are aimed at realization. The New Age processes are created from the intensity, streaming, from the understanding that emotion has no place.

Understanding means balancing, calibrating energy to the midline, seeing the future and seeing insights. The intention is to understand growth processes through the present and envisaging the future.

When a person understands his road and acts with righteousness, he can form an energetic summon and create a reality on various subjects that are very important to him. For example: Relationships - he equalizes the frequency between his life and his mate's life, from a wide range of parameters that constitute a common path to growth.

A relationship is a successful example of creating a reality that is supposed to be the mindset in every person's life. The creation of reality embeds a future to a human life and pulls it forward with the thought directed on doing.

When a person is in a state of constant action and understanding, he does not sit idly by. He is busy working, busy with realization, and is preoccupied with seeing the future. Recollect the emotionally related understandings of the previous age, when a person had no vision and he did not see a future - he established emotions emanating from his inner turmoil. He formed within himself frustration, incomprehension and weakness to a sense of defeat, and thus, out of weakness, he established the control and domination of fear and darkness in his life. These created the inner turmoil, and the person felt that he is halted and not progressing with his life.

When a person remains idle, does nothing, thus, promoted an inner turmoil, he loses his inner strength. He loses his self. His life was about doing and giving to others, through will and need to receive attention or love. He did everything for his surroundings, but did hardly anything for himself.

But in the New Age, we ask you to change your past thinking and begin to see your future as you wish to see it. You can choose to be idle for a certain amount of time, but do so knowing that this idleness must be temporary and that the whole process must be temporary.

Know how to set time in Creation and see a future because if you do not see your future, you will not know how to apply the creation of reality and connect to the realms of darkness, lack of understanding and purpose, and connect to the inner pain that was part of you in previous life.

The thin line between being happy and being sad or depressed is the blink of an eye. From the point at which a person decides to stop sitting idly by, and decides to make a difference. This is the moment when he will raise himself and his life and gallop ahead. The moment that a person chooses to remove his foot from the gas pedal of life, this is the moment he will lose his power - never forget it.

A person who has inner strength and vision, has a meaning to success. But when the power is taken away from the person, he will feel how his energy is withdrawn from him. It feels like a dying battery. And just like in electrical appliances, when the battery is running low, the output of the device decreases.

Therefore, to preserve the vitality of your life to remain full and yielding, envisaging your future always is important. See the vision, see the growth, see the processes of your life, not for your family members, not for your children, but for yourself only.

When you give your soul to your children and to the home and family processes - you waste most of the energy in your body, and the vision has almost nothing left. Your energetic power is weakening and you do not have the inner powers to see the future and the path to the future. That way you lose the power that surrounds you, and you do not always know why. You lose your strength because you did not distribute it correctly. Because you have given most of your energy and attention to others, and you have forgotten yourself, it is a gross and blatant violation of self-love.

In the New Age, self-love is of high importance because self-love is created in the human mind, and self-love opens his eyes to the meaning of growth through insights.

When a person loves himself, he places himself first by listening to himself and out of a desire to succeed and see a future. Self-love causes a person not to remain idle and seek incentives to create meanings in his life.

Self-love makes a person think about what he does for himself, how he improves himself and how he increases his energetic power - this is an energetic summon.

The meaning of life is the constant thinking of how to improve yourself, how to create power in your life, how to motivate the engines of action. This is the meaning of life and creation of reality. It is a general understanding that you, as a human being, when you conduct yourself rightfully, your life is illuminated and run through accelerated processes.

For example, when you drive a car and you go down a slippery-slope, you do not need to press the gas pedal. You let the engine accelerate itself by the power of inertia. This is the meaning you need to understand when you create reality.

You are not supposed to be constantly thinking of how to create reality, because you are using the **element of fire** and you can also exhaust yourself or consume precious energy resources and end up "burning" yourself in vain. This is how you can also lose hope. This is not the goal. As far as we are concerned, the goal to create set times when you do not bring your thought into constant thinking. It is not right.

From time to time, send an understanding to Creation so that it would not forget you. This is how you create a reality from the scenario of your life. Explain to Creation what is it that you want exactly, and remind it that you want to succeed, create understandings on how you want to succeed. Do it as a different energetic summon. This is the way and this is the creation of reality, and it does not matter if you create a small comma or you create a whole world.

For you, the most important path, is the path of action. When you act, you are not idle. When you act, you are living out of a constant vision. It is your job to see the ultimate goal and to remind Creation from time to time, that you have not forgotten your dreams and that you wish to realize them.

You need to know and understand that your guides sometimes give you bonuses along the road, like small gifts of abundance, so that you will strengthen your faith in your road in yourself. They give you gifts in the form of people they introduce you, or gifts that you are supposed to receive "just like that," so that the understanding will create a reinforcement within you, without defeat, through a contact with your guides.

The connection to the creation of reality originates in creative thought and creation that stem from the **element of air**. This is the important connection that will propel you in your life through a process of great light.

There is a very high meaning to understanding your existential life, what do you want to change, and how do you seek to improve the existing and create a future. This is what you do when you do not sit idly by, while seeing the future pulls you forward and prevents your emotions from taking over.

Understand, you are here on the **seam line** that creates the thin line between light and darkness. In one minute, you can reach levels of light, and in another, you can reach levels of darkness. This is what you do by creative thought and a reality-creation thought. Precisely because of the sensitivity of the New Age, you need to be aware of the realms of darkness, and you must not let darkness take over your life anymore.

We know that you are in constant struggles between the realms of light and the realms of darkness, and we know that these constant struggles have a severe impact on your life. We know that it is difficult for you, but the only way to separate from the realms of darkness, is to connect with us and be calibrated to the goal, to see the future and to create the reality of your life.

Therefore, we recommend that you create in your life understandings of all the phases that you go through along the way, and when you walk in these phases, you will feel that your actions are not conducted in vain.

We suggest that you record the processes that you are experiencing, and over time, you will see how these processes were created for you.

This is how you will see later, that everything that you sought, fulfilled itself almost completely.

And if you look over your shoulder, you will realize that you have come a long way in the road of change and understanding. You will understand that every phase that you ingrained with meaning, has connected you to high powers and energy of hope. This energy encourages you not to give up. It inspires you not to connect with the realms of darkness, guarding you in its own way, and connecting you to simplicity.

Your great gift on the way is the realization. When you create the reality of your life, you feel lucky, and luck does not just come randomly, it is a luck that also connects you to your guides. Along the way you write, you ask the guides, ask yourself, and you receive understandings and guidance. The Creation, that sees that you are doing the right thing, creates a realization for you.

Not always does a person know or able to ask the guides, or himself, whether he acted correctly. But do not worry, in these situations, the subconscious connects with you. It is what keeps you from falling again into the realms of darkness. The subconscious reverberates in your thoughts positive points by recollection, reminding you that when the dark world was part of your life in past incarnations, the fear took over. But when you are connected to the light, your soul protects you and reinforces you along the way. In this process, you will feel that something in your life is changing and your life is becoming more meaningful and happier.

Feel how you live by the fire energy that burns in your world. An energy of excitement that is pulsing inside you,

An energy of action that seeks your benefit. And when that energy exists within you, you will see that joy of life becomes part of you and an energy of will and need for action is connected to you.

Your existential deed also restores the light processes and distances the dark realms from your life.

When thoughts, emotions, difficulties and suffering are removed from your life, you operate through a significant realization of light and growth processes. And this is the stream of life that is combined with the creation of reality.

When light processes are calibrated within you during the creation of reality, they are more structured and connect you to your goal easily. We will help you create growth processes, help you through understandings of frequency and from words. We will help and guide you, in the creation of the reality of your life. Let us start:

FREQUENCY TREATMENT

See a white ray of light descends from heaven.

See the ray of white light enters you, passing through the chakras in your body, and illuminating each energy center with its color:

- **Crown (purple)**
- **The third eye (indigo)**
- **Throat (blue)**
- **Heart (green)**
- **Solar plexus (yellow). Please note, if there are feelings in this energy center, reduce them completely.**
- **The ray of white light continues down to the Sacral chakra (orange), and up to the Root chakra (red).**

Breathe and watch every illuminated chakra, with every energy center connected to the other by the beam of white light from the Crown to the Root chakra.

Breathe and feel how each breath diffuses the white light energy into every cell of your body.

Feel how the body connects to a sense of calm and serenity from a process of balance.

Cleanse your mind of any thought, and remove from the golden triangle (throat, heart, and solar plexus chakras), any emotion that hinders you from cleansing your body.

See your entire body painted white, with all the chakras painted, each with its color.

Breathe and feel how the beam of white light fills you with the energy of renewal from head to toe.

If you feel any pain in your body, now is time to send a ray of light and treat that pain.

We want your body to be calm, relaxed and ready to accept.

Keep breathing.

We are back again, clean your mind of any thought. We are now connecting you to high consciousness in the Crown chakra (purple) and the Third eye chakra (indigo)

(These two upper chakras are responsible for the energetic summons of growth processes).

Feel your body cleansed, relaxed and ready to accept change processes.

Focus on your thought, your mind, and see your future.

Create goals, create understanding, you choose what you want to receive.

Convey what your future must be.

See how you live your future... try to imagine a picture.

See it as a script, like a movie, to the ultimate goal.

When you imagine and see, you open your heart to understanding and believing in success.

Through the supernatural vision, you create a reality and give life to this reality.

As a result of the process, feel satisfied and happy with the script you see.

Feel a sense of simplicity that nothing bothers you.

Breathe and feel connected.

See yourself satisfied and ready to discharge anything that is disturbing you to achieve your goal - see the result again.

Be goal-oriented, feel that your frequency is clean and no emotion or thought enters, other than the creation of the reality of your life.

Feel that your body is ready to contain, accept, and is not resisting.

See how the ray of white light returns to the sky and you stay with the memory that is engraved in your mind, when your whole body is still flooded with a white energy of hope.

Remember:

You need to see and remind yourself nothing but the goal,

Remind yourself the road and the outcome you choose to create meaning,

And preserve an image in your mind that is intended to remind you the outcome from time to time.

Thank you.

LESSON 9
THE FREQUENCY OF JOY

In your developmental way, you must connect joy to your life.

When you talk about the creation of reality and the meaning of life as a reality, you need to understand that when joy has no love, no pleasure, no path or foresight - you cannot create reality.

Reality is created out of joy, desire and hope. When there is joy in a person, it creates within him, patience and latitude, and opens the spatial vision.

When a person lacks joy, then sadness, frustration and darkness enter and create pain in his mind. When a person lives through lack of joy, his inner mourning creates a meaning.

We repeat these understandings with the knowledge that you do know them, but we want to reinforce them you to enlighten you and your consciousness - you have the understanding, the way and the realization to breakthrough.

If you understand the meaning of life, and you know that from the meaning of life you connect with your inner self, create family, the family foundation and a proper relationship - you understand that all these are accompanying you and leading you to happiness.

If you look at your life, you will see that it does not exist out of ordinary consciousness, just to live life monotonously or routinely. As you have understood, this routine is bad, and the human soul needs experiences. The human soul is happy and joyful when you are aroused and stimulate it with experiences.

When you connect, from within yourself, to your inner self, and you do it through high understanding and connection to the Light of Creation, the path you take is through growth.

Growth is not conducted out of monotony. It is conducted out of desire and joy, the need to awaken and illuminate your soul. When a soul is stimulated, it wants to constantly act through joy and from the stimulus of the **element of fire**, because the **element of fire** stimulates action.

When a person is motivated by the **element of fire**, the **element of fire** creates frustration and understanding of the connection to darkness. You already know that the emotional difficulties arise when there is a flooding of the elements of fire water. Low water has no existence (we elaborated about it previously), and the fire is also supposed to be transformed into a state of action. That is, to connect to the living, to connect to the action, to connect to the understandings of the meaning of life. You do that with the **element of fire**.

You need to create the **element of fire** and connect it to the element of high air, because these are the leading frequencies in the New Age.

The role of the **element of fire** and the **element of air** is to motivate the person, create essence, convey his thought or creativity, and be the first in every process. This is what you see in the start-up companies you have discovered in recent years.

Start-up companies are motivated by the **element of fire** and the element of high air, and their role is to motivate, seek, discover, awake and create excitement.

The internal burning of the action, stems from the **element of fire** and derives from joy. When a person feels inner joy, he connects to happiness, and to the internal stimulus that speaks of happiness.

A happy man does not connect to the low water. He connects only to action because he understands from his subconscious that action has a very high meaning to separate from the realms of darkness.

The action in your world is manifested when a person is active and preoccupied with thought and vision, and creates the desire to act.

We give you tools to separate from the dark realms, so that you will understand that it is very important to be active all the time since action is the burning that is created by the **element of air** and the desire to act, so that the soul will blossom and illuminate, through high understanding, the meaningful way by which you live.

Growth processes are manifested from the meaning of the joy that arises from the **element of fire**. A person who wants something for his life, connects to the inner need that derives from joy. A person who chooses to understand, understands out of a desire that is accompanied by joy. He opens his understandings, and these help him choose the right path that will create a meaning and existence in his life.

This is also the case in a relationship. When a person chooses joy, he chooses the right mate to create his inner joy, and from this, he also chooses to bring children to the world, who are supposed to enlarge his family and create joy in his life. From the family foundation, joy is created which leads to the creation of a great happiness. This accompanies a person like the emanation of streaming foundation that creates the circularity of life.

When the cycle of life streams continuously and does not cause difficulty, it creates understanding and connection to happiness. It creates processes to make sure that a good person will feel happy because he feels that his life is linked to what is right.

We expect that when you are connected to the New Age, through the right growth processes, you will reach an understanding that will connect you to the element of high air.

When you choose to act, the action connects you to the process through desire, inner burning and fire. You express your soul in a productive activity when you are connected to the element of high water, which expresses creation within you.

The balance and meaning in your life are built from the **element of earth**. You already know that the meaning of life has a considerable understanding of balance, that the life of a balanced person is created from hope and the march forward.

If you look at your life, you will see that the difficulty (emotion) anchored them. The difficulty clouded your soul and created a meaning of the negative **element of earth** in your life. Thus, the frustration increased, and the internal feelings of guilt stemmed from a lack of self-regard. You feel that you gave others and did not give yourself. This process created a turmoil within you because you "wasted" a lot of energy to satisfy others, and feel a reluctance to keep acting. In fact, you feel that the battery of your life is running out and was wasted on nonsense. However, you did not understand and did not know how to behave differently. You did not know how to make the change.

When you are motivated by high emotion, you know that the creational abundance is open for you. The processes create a path that opens your mind and break through your boundaries. This is how you are grateful for the life you have received.

When you connect directly to the **element of air** and the element of high water - it calibrates you to high understandings and connect you to the creation of reality of your life. They create within you, the inner joy, happiness and everything that drives your life in the process of development.

You know that a happy person feels enriched. Within himself, he feels rich. He feels that his interior is rich and balanced by the four elements. He feels lucky and that the universe, abundance and life itself, are opening for him and all he needs to do is walk in whatever path he chooses.

When a person feels that abundance and roads are open for him, this is the stage at which happiness also connects to it. He feels that he is not alone, he feels that creation is beside him and creates meaning with him. He feels that he is following his path of life and is doing right. Thus, joy also connects to him because he understands that the road, the action and the very life, are breaking open for him, and all he needs to do is to realize it. Through realization, he connects to the joy that arises within him, reinforces and intensifies itself at any given moment.

He connects to the joy and says to himself: "I am open to receive." Through this sense, he also opens the realms of abundance in the universe. And when the universe sees that man is acting right and through high emotion, high thinking, and the right choices and joy - the universe elevates him to a higher frequency and expands his consciousness.

When a person knows that he is acting correctly, his joy surpasses fear. A happy man does not let fear enter his life and fail him. A happy man, who acts out of joy, knows that Creation is on his side and helps him grow. He knows inside that he is not alone.

And a person who is confident that he is not alone, does not connect with darkness, he connects to joy processes, growth and realization. He breaks boundaries and does not understand how these things happen to him, but he understands that these processes merge from inner trust and faith that stream from him, and from his interaction with creation.

A person who attaches himself inwardly, conveys the meaning of happiness. The human soul is preoccupied with questions: If I do this and that, will I be happy? How can I transcend and be happy?

When talking about happiness, the human mind remembers, from the collective memory that dwells within the cosmic library, darkness processes. These rectifications and difficulties are the result of previous incarnations. The collective memory that it accumulates, is incomprehension and writhing in your various stages of life. But you are today in the crossroads of a New Age, and the New Energy is coming to teach you (even though you live in the age of earth), how to think from the **element of air** that is supposed to exist in the next age.

You can understand and the developmental ability to open your world to another vision. You have reached a stage and you are teaching your consciousness how to connect to the energy and frequency of the New Age.

It does not matter that your body, your vessel, is in the present age.

Your consciousness belongs to the New Age.

Your thinking works according to the power of the New Age.

Your life runs in the pace of the New Age.

You become spiritual teachers and teach others how to behave. In any situation, you introduce positive thought processes that stem from understanding and joy. Thus, through your behavior, you teach others to behave differently within the energy of the New Age, and you do so subconsciously.

The human soul will always see darkness because it remembers incarnations. But as you know, at the launch points of the New Age, the soul creates a switch for different thinking, and it brings people to places that will teach them how to change. In its way, the soul creates an inner stimulus within people, to teach us how to change. When a person learns how to change (considering all the processes he has undergone in his life), he calibrates his thought to look at life from another perspective and from the new frequencies of the New Age.

In his mind, he calibrates his vision of the future vision, when his body remains in the past. The thought slowly connects the vessel - the body, to a process of balancing through the four elements, and also teaches the body how to accommodate the new frequencies.

When you understand, the new frequencies and insights slowly seep into the cells of your body. Your life changes as you think - it is the flow that gathers all the processes you created, and conveys the meanings of anchoring.

Anchoring for you, is the process of joy, because joy opens your hearts and your consciousness. You learn to accept that the understanding that creation is on your side.

Trust and faith are made out of a process of joy. When a person believes that his life is filled with abundance and joy, and the family and the relationship he choses are the best for him, when he stops delving into negative and in difficulty processes and delves only into the positive processes - abundance connects to his life and makes him happy.

If a person decides to accept his or her mate for a shared life, this understanding must be based on a vision of the future. A person needs to understand that he must not connect to negativity, but rather to moments of desire for a shared life and vision of the future. Embrace the moments of joy that you have created and the mutual understandings, and create a future, for a future combined with moments of joy, creates hope of continuity.

The vision of the future creates points of contact for erasing past insights. It erases deficiencies that created internal chaos, and erases situations in which the person feels that he is willing to give up past processes - where emotion overshadowed joy and pushed him to connect to realms of perpetual darkness.

When the person conveys the meaning of joy that comes from his thought - his future may be easier. From this understanding point, the emotion is prevented from creating a painful weight that stems from a negative **element of earth**, and thus, only through will, awareness and understanding, can a person connect to joy.

Remember, you chose your parents, your family and your mates, for growth only. You chooses whether to grow through envisaging the future and connecting to joy, or staying behind - **If you choose a process of joy, the understanding of the process may connect you to a constant joy that stems from the mindset of creating the reality of your life.**

When you decide to choose to be joyful and happy, you transpire that energy to Creation as well. And when it sees your joy, it feels that your shared path is safe.

You must remember to be happy because a person's tendency, in his thoughts, is to always go back to emotional states. In this behavior, he lays stones on his path and closes the opportunities that face him.

At a certain point, a person stops connecting to difficulty processes and misunderstanding, and realizes that he cannot change his life. His life is open to eternal joy. Even if he dwells in states of difficulty, he knows how to cast them aside. He knows that the difficulty is part of his life, but he does not let it cloud his life.

Creation sees in you the potential of people who can progress without stopping. In the New Age, the meaning of happiness is to move forward without a stop.

If you connect to the **element of fire** and the **element of air**, your life may be like a marathon. However, you must follow your own pace, not the pace that Creation dictates to you. Since you are at the beginning of an age, you dictate the pace, but the pace means that you will not go back. Do not let the past manifest within you, the meaning of going back. You must march forward through a massive development and foresight. Thus, Creation opens the potentials for every person it knows that is taking the right path.

We repeat: Do not worry. Thus, with a renewed thought, we open and change your consciousness, and open your eyes to the growth processes. We do not let your thought create a mirage. Our repetitive words create a kind of mental fixation.

Our words serve as your tailwind.

Our words tell you not to be afraid to depart from the difficulty.

Our words tell you to connect to growth processes and not be afraid to depart from the realms of darkness.

Do not be afraid to leave them behind. Do not be afraid, they create unnecessary stress in your life.

Do not be afraid to look forward to all the potential doors, and do not be afraid to create meaning out of growth processes.

Do not be afraid to look forward to your life and connect to the essence of joy.

Do not be afraid to step up in frequency and develop spiritually, because your role in the meaning of life, is to connect to great happiness, to connect to constant action, and to connect to the essence of eternal worldview.

Do not sit idly by, and do not wait for your mate to come with you. No, you must follow your path, your existence, your understanding, for the will of the soul, is yours alone.

You pave the road, and whoever wants to follow, will come later or be left behind. Not always, the same soul fit into your new life, and not always, your happiness will be the happiness of others. Your will is not always the same will of others.

Sometimes you start your life out of an equation line or out of some rectifications, and sometimes even these rectifications do not create equality in your life, because emotion impedes you from succeeding. If you want and need to succeed, you need (at least in your thinking), to set your emotion free.

We do not tell you to complete the family process, if it does not suit you.

We say that you, in your inner essence, need to put your inner happiness, your soul happiness, and the joy within you, at the center of the stage.

Joy is important. It is important for growth processes in your life, it is important for magnetizing processes, it is important for stream processes, and when there is joy in you, you also emit this joy on your family. Thus, through joy, you also awaken others who will connect with you along the way.

Once you cloak the difficult situations with joy, the lack of communication "have a feast." For the meaning of life, in terms of primary understanding, is proper communication. And for you to be happy, you need to use the communication and convey yourself through it, rather than keeping things bolted up within you. You must create a meaning of flow, create a meaning of growth, and convey the meanings of light.

When your soul is illuminated, your life is illuminated. You radiate your encompassing happiness. From the connection to the high, from high insights and open heavenly channels - you also connect those who are close to you, to the joy processes.

We expect that when you understand the mindset that Creation asks of you, you will open your eyes to new growth processes.

We expect that when you understand the meaning of your life, you will understand that it is of great importance, before the processes and the connection to all the understandings that we given you, are implemented. There is an existential understanding of your great happiness, and when you connect to joy, you connect to infinite possibilities and the stream of life comes to you at any given moment.

In your soul, you will feel the joy that emanates from the solar plexus because it connects you to the desire and creativity that are located in the two lower chakras.

All the joy is supposed to come from your inner stomach, the stomach that creates simplicity, understanding and insight.

The joy in your life will connect you to high consciousness and convey a sense of growth.

Understand, your life is important and meaningful to us, and your life should be a life that connects you to learning. When you learn, we also learn.

We look at you and see you as the first swallows of growth processes linked to the New Age. Your road, like the cars and locomotives of the first trains in a whole creational railway station, will mean freedom to others as well.

We, in Creation, can also create, through understanding, needs and desires in others. We can manifest meaning in them so that they too, will connect to light processes and abundance processes. They will notice it on you. When you connect to joy processes, they will see you and will also want joy in their lives.

They see your existence, and that is where you choose to be. This is the place where you, through inner faith, through creation of reality, open your world.

You can create a reality of materiality and reality of understanding, but if joy does not exist within you, you cannot create your personal reality. In your personal reality, where family, children and friends exist, is the place at which you need to be connected to happiness.

A joyful and happy man magnetizes others to him. If you magnetize success, success has no emotion. If you magnetize a property, the property has no emotion. But if you live with your family, and you are not joyful and happy - realization will have no value.

If there is no one to which you want to convey your realization, and no one which you create materiality for - the realization of materiality will not have value. You have created materiality for you, but how much material do you need?

A person who gives to his family and gives to others, happiness returns to him like a boomerang, through high emotion and inner joy.

Growth stems from shared understanding processes and vision of processes, and from the theoretical understandings that you route in your mind. As long as you are connected to high emotion and high understanding - your path of life will lead you forward with joy and realization. When your life realizes itself through light processes, your existence will be true.

Be blessed with the growth processes of your life

Put your existence on the front of the stage - the stage of your life

Where you will convey an inclusive meaning and a collective meaning

That stem from growth processes, happiness, joy and light

LESSON 10
IMPLEMENTATION AND REALIZATION

Dear souls, you have created a wonderful way of connecting to Creation, and a wonderful path that brings you a whole world of insights.

As you expand your consciousness and look at the world around you, notice how your life slowly open like an expanding green meadow. The different developmental thinking is leading you forward. This is the path to your fulfillment and implementation.

The spiritual development will connect you to a high understanding, a developing aura and a supreme abundance, and when you understand, your insights create a development within you. Your insights remove your defensive walls and fears, and prompt you to be open and aware of the process that creates a rebirth in your life. The breakthrough occurs within your own world.

A breakthrough occurs when a person feels that realization is in his veins and his life is meant to express and convey something. His evolution and breakthrough show that he is ripe for action, ready for a headway and fulfillment, but his life is at a standstill. When your life is halted, you feel the **element of fire** boiling. It is a creational trigger of an awakening call to understanding.

You need to understand that creation is about provoking existence in a person. When a person seeks a headway in his life, he must connect to the understandings obtained from the **element of fire**. Sometimes a person feels that the understandings he receives are like a hot potato coming out of the oven. Meaning, he sees that the product does exist, but it is difficult for him to connect to it.

When a person acts with the intention of future growth, he understand that it is important to be connected to the energy of the New Age. This should be seared within him because the high energy helps him connect to the path and to every process, like a feeling of water streaming in the river.

In other words, you must send the "treasure box" that Creation implanted within you. The "treasure" is the road that you follow, and the water in the river means that you need to try to adjust your energy to the rhythm of others' lives. Others may feel fear when you burst into a closed door.

Not every person has the understandings to reach his destiny, and not every person can implement the processes he understands he must do. But the meaning of your life is that you must be connected to a life of happiness, a peaceful life, and a perfect life. Something in the process of your life needs to express itself through the growth processes of a "treasure box" that sails on the river.

And this box is the positive Pandora box you are meant to connect to. This is the significant Pandora box you can always open and use the tools you received, for the stream of life. Inside the Pandora's box are the insights that Creation has given you, but the stream of life is yours because this box is yours. You can open it and use it at your own pace.

When a person is connected to the state of mind of the New Age, he develops and evolves. On his way, he also develops others: his surrounding, his family and his children. The pace should be within the stream of your life because that is the will of your soul. But if you arrive to your surrounding like a stormy wind, you will feel that you lose the effect, and the gilded Pandora's Box may also sink. Then ask yourself sadly, why did you have to go through the whole process. You may even feel that the process was not necessary at all because you feel that your life is sinking and all the spiritual development has created a difficulty for you.

You have the Ace card in your deck of cards. The Ace is the spiritual development that you have created in your life and may serve you at moments when your insight and consciousness is about to create and implement in your life.

The frequencies of the world are ups and downs. A person may feel that sometimes he is down and sometimes he feels elevated. Every person, wherever he may be, lives with pulses of ups and downs. But your awareness creates meaning and understandings why a person feels that his energy has declined. Your awareness also knows how a person can lift himself up. You have the tools to do this and they are the "treasure box" that you carry in your life.

But others, who do not have these tools, may feel threatened by your power, your spirit and your way of thinking. They may feel the desire and the need to create a development in their lives, but they will be afraid to board the train or even to arrive at the train station and wait for their destined train. They will think that spiritual development and the need for a change, are negative processes.

There are people in the world whose negative thoughts are so strong and so meaningful that their vision for the future cannot always sense the positive experience. But it is in your hands (from walking between the drops and from the creation of meanings) to know, to understand and to prompt others to create a realization for themselves. You feel them and you can pick them up, and inject them with insights. They are drawn to your frequency, but your frequency should be pliable and not constrained.

When you are looking to grow in your life, you need to visualize your progress, goals, your future, your meaning and your growth. When you see goals, you create the reality of your life and connect to abundance and simplicity.

Your surroundings may understand the path of your life and see your growth processes as meaningful. They do not always show this but they understand the implications of this development, because they learn through you, how to achieve development processes and change. But you are the one who pulls the strings because you are connected to the energy of a stream that creates awareness in your life. From this energy, you create the reality of your life, for you understand that your path of life is to be accompanied by common growth of many souls that will go with you, especially the souls around you.

You can choose to be the locomotive in any field that you choose: in relationships, in parenthood, in friendships, at work, in development and anything you choose to grow with and express a meaning. This is done through the charisma that connects to your body, and the energy that you created with it, brings a meaning. From understanding of your right to choose and from the bonus you created when you became part of growth processes. From understanding of survival, of how to avoid low places. This is because you realize that your soul is not good at being in the dark.

When your soul seeks to create development, this process begins in heaven. Imagine that heaven opens for you like a wish and like rain on a clear day, which connects you with the light of the sun and cleanses the air that overshadows misunderstanding.

Your world, the world you live in, can be in a process of growth, understanding and meaning. Your existence is created when you realize that the reason you came into this world is to be happy.

In other words, you have come to this world to create the connection with Creation and to follow the will of Creation. This is the way to unload all the burden of darkness and difficulty from your life. And out of simplicity you connect to the understanding of the high frequency and New Age energy.

When in life you understand and familiar with the tools, you know how to make yourself happy.

You are happy in your relationship, happy with yourself, happy with your family, happy with your friends, happy with the path and with the tools you have received, and happy that you have the power and the energy to be the locomotive and lead the others on the train of life.

Creation seeks to connect many understanding to a person. A person does not always understand that it is in his own hands to create connection and realization.

When a person is connected to Creation, he understands that he can break the difficulty and unload the burdens he feels in his life. He works through patience and tolerance, knows how to connect with himself and his soul correctly, so that the soul will know how to spread the light and the energy and expand its aura.

When your aura is broad, the meaning of your life is that you do not limit yourself. You do not clip your wings along the way, and you act out of the growth foundation of development.

The mindset of your life leads you to a new understanding. It leads you to the inner faith and the daring that you are truly a creature of Creation. That you are truly being led by a proper action. That your role here is to function, to implement and to realize, and that is how you connect to happiness.

When you function, act and connect to action, Creation connects with every part of the life you have created. When you want a relationship, for example, you must turn the world upside down and wish with all your heart to have a relationship and connect it to your life.

And for those who have a relationship, you must do the maximum to preserve the shared space through understandings of growth and energy.

When you seek to implement the idea of a happy family, rather than a family that is in a state of an emotional meltdown, you can create the growth processes, with the understanding and proper energy of open thinking, rather than set thinking from past conventions.

When you act and apply through light processes, you connect yourself to your inner self and to a proper inner relationship. And when you live in peace with your inner self, you are filled with power and emotional resilience and can move forward.

It is very important for a person to know how to implement processes, so he understand that the real reason he has come to the world is to be happy. This is how he realizes that the more he nullifies the realms of emotion and the realms of rectifications, the more he will be connected to the essence of happiness.

A person must understand that he must enjoy all the little things that happiness connects to him through implementation and realization.

If a person wants to be happy but does nothing to obtain it, happiness will never knock on his door.

Happiness comes to a person only through realization, application and action, as well as the fact that a person does not sit idly by, that he can connect all the insights he received from Creation, since he understands that they suit him.

Not every insight is appropriate for every person, not every job is suitable for every person, and not every mission is the right mission for every person. Every person is an individual and can create his own developments. You already know that and we reinforce it within you.

We want you to understand the meaning of realization, meaning of implementation and the meaning of existence. We want you to understand the meaning of being drawn into emptiness and darkness. If a person does not find his place, he can easily return to the state he once was.

When a person does not act, does not realize, does not initiate, does not function and does not expand the realms of his mind and his consciences – darkness will take him back to his dwelling as his prisoner.

Your job is to understand that when you have reached the world of light, you have come into the world with which you are developing. As you develop and open your consciousness, the world of light becomes familiar and occupies an important place in your life. You have the power and understanding to eradicate the realms of darkness that will not connect with you again. The realms of darkness can be a public domain, but within you, you need to understand and decide that you do not dwell in this place anymore.

Your growth may arise and emerge from a new path. From being able to look and see that you can create the vibrations of your life. Imagine a stone thrown into the water and creating ripples. You can be the stone that creates the ripples of the waves, because in your existence, you need to rise and evolve. You must decide what you want to do in your life, and how you are going to create and realize your life.

Everyone needs to know, understand, and remember, that Creation has its own time. And when you are in the process of doing your work, sometimes Creation wants to see how strong you are, how much you create meaning and understanding along the way. It wants to see that you are not giving up, but on the contrary - that you are determined to set out and become the stone that creates the ripples of the waves upon the water.

Creation wants to see how much you understand the importance of patience and tolerance in your life. Creation has its time and it cannot always stand by you when you want its help. Patience and tolerance mean forbearance that leads to spiritual growth and development. This understanding has an important meaning in your life.

When a person begins his rectifications, he starts them out of incomprehension, frustration, and internal chaos that stem from the **element of fire**. The inner chaos increases the sound levels, increases the discomfort and the high octaves that others cannot hear and that creates a sense of difficulty which raises new walls and other rectifications.

When you live your life, you need to understand that patience and tolerance have a significant power upon which you may live your life. Sometimes it is difficult to do this, because you feel that your consciousness is expanding within the Solar Plexus chakra, and the nerves and tensions create incomprehension within.

Understand, you can also control all the energy centers and not let them breach the line of balance. You can open your mind and understand why things happen, and understand what happens to other people. You do it out of empathy, out of tolerance and with understanding that there are other people who are drifting with you down the streams of life.

By understanding others, you are preventing yourself from connecting to a sense of inner chaos and other rectifications. You have the insights and abilities to sense them and to understand your own path of life. When you understand and create patience and tolerance within, you feel exaltation. This, too, is a spiritual development.

But remember, not everyone has a positive Pandora box full of insights, understandings, a connection to New Age energy, proper thinking and a significant toolbox for life.

Not everyone who has an energetic decline, can use the tools he received for the stream of life. Not everyone connects to insights to seek meaning, and not everyone has the insight to look at life and to understand that there is something stronger that tells him, "I am here to help you advance forward."

It is us, your guides, who connect you to insights and supply your tailwind. We convey the meaning of progress and create within you, understandings and insights of development, of lifting your head high, of strengthening, of expressing your opinion and creating growth. We reinforce your inner personality to convey the meaning of your path, understanding, and development.

That is how you empower your inner personality. That is how everyone else will feel the change in you and want to connect with the new person that is created - you. They will look upon you, see you in a new light and realize that you have changed and lead a new course of. But remember, the realizing is in your hands - you are the locomotive.

Please understand, not everyone can be a locomotive, and not everyone can be the one who pulls the train of his life forward. There are those who still feel that they are driven by emotion and incomprehension that play a significant part in their lives. But the person who chooses to create spiritual development, chooses to understand his new world with enlightened thought and a new path, realizes that the balance created in his life is good for him. He feels that inner cleanliness has created a meaning of growth and connected it to the four balanced elements.

Realization and implementation begin when the four elements are balanced:

When the clear thought of the **element of air** sees growth and goals, when the **element of earth** is grounded and connected to insights of action and development, when the **element of water** creates the high emotion and when the inner burning - the **element of fire** - is burning for action stemming from growth.

All four elements are connected to you when you feel balanced. Once you understand a process and you create a meaning, you connect to the right balance.

These understandings come together like a magnet that magnetizes all the particles missing in your mind. These processes create a balance in your life from the realization and implementation of processes that magnetize the missing pieces that are important to your growth.

We welcome you, and create within you an open way from righteous understandings and tailwind that will create within you emotional understanding support when you go about your way of life.

We are sending you forward to the implementation and realization from intentions and understandings, that you choose to be there. In your new way of your life we tell you:

- **Every thought that is rolling through your mind now, creates with you, the meaning of success.**

- **Every thought you are supposed to express, creates understandings and insights of growth.**

- **Any understanding that you decide to implement, realize and perform, is successful for you.**

- **You operate with a high understanding of the connection, which stems from balance and an inner belief, that you are indeed connected to us.**

We, your guides, are sending you out to independence,

And know how to connect to the realms that you choose,

And to convey meaning.

We wish upon you that you may know how to create the eternal foundation of happiness of your life,

So that you can understand the importance of your life and give them the importance of realization.

Most importantly, you must understand the real reason you have come to the world.

Because your soul has already chosen you.

It wants you to be happy.

We congratulate you,

Embrace you and open a new door with you.

Get out and start your life

From high insights and from a meaningful connection of infinity.

Thank you.

QUESTIONS AND ANSWERS

Why does the knowledge end after ten lessons? Is this significant?

When we gave the ten lessons of the meaning of life, we created in you the insights just as the Ten Commandments were given to the people of Israel in Egypt.

We are not creating here a renewed Matan Torah (the giving of the Torah), but rather a renewed giving of insights. The rules of the game and the rules of the insights are known to every human being. But not every human being is prepared to understand and to convey with them meaning of growth processes and connection.

A person knows every commandment and the spirit in which these pronouncements were given.

A person lives his life through the drive to live, not through the desire to break the insights open. The game rules were given to people who wish to create meaning, to be open to insights, and to enhance their state of mind.

The meaning of life is to be happy and end difficulty processes and rectifications. A person knows what the difficulty processes and rectifications are, but a person's realization should also be in the insight.

And here **The Meaning of Life** emanates from that moment when a person feels that he knows everything, his fields of study open and he feels that he wants to continue creating insights.

The Meaning of Life connects all the ends of the insights within those who have begun spiritual development processes. It connects the person to the insights and gives meaning of change and engagement. The ten rules are rules of insight alone, of opening to reality.

Sometimes those who read **The Meaning of Life** will know that the role of this knowledge is to create understandings, and sometimes a person will feel stimulated and will know that he wants to understand more and will begin to create a process of spiritual development and to cope with various problems that cloud his personal happiness, and use other means of knowledge that may help him.

Today when you are in the age of the **seam line**, you need to convey the meaning of growth, development and openness, open your consciousness and care for it. You need to enhance the senses and characters that you want to end. To enhance through understanding that a person wants to end a process, and once he ended the process, he wants to move forward and feel balanced.

A person's soul wishes to connect to happiness; it does not want to create meanings of difficulty. A person's soul wishes to live in openness and development because that is its way. The person's role is to know how to put his finger on the little loose ends of the puzzles that did not want to turn over in his life, puzzles of states of difficulty and misunderstanding, and you have the tools with which to convey meaning.

A person needs no more. He does not need to develop and understand what is happening in heaven and what is happening in Creation.

He wants to cope with his life from the "here" and "now", out of his emotional roots. This is how he realizes that he must create the balance between the four elements. From this place there will be growth, creation, meaning and happiness in his life.

Creating spiritual development is a process that sometimes takes time and is often tiring, especially since the results are not evident immediately. What do we say to someone who feels that way?

We, the guides, create the tailwind for a person, and support him when he follows the right path. When he puts up his hands in defeat, we come to him and give him a gentle push so that he is empowered and will connect to the **element of air** and the other three elements in his life, to be balanced.

When we convey meaning, we create hope within him.

However, when these processes are impeded, the person feels defeat and loss of purpose: his body contracts, his shoulders fall, his vision snaps and sometimes the goal also seems distant.

Even if the person feels that the processes are postponed, he is meant to connect to hope for he needs to understand that his path is correct. In every person's mind, there is the mindset of the goal and a vision of the future. A person needs to see the future and feel how the high energy is connected to it through his insights. That energy belongs to the New Age.

And when the goal connects, it brings the person to hope, connects him to simplicity and creates a softness and understanding. The goal opens his mind, reduces his frustration, encourages him through a positive energetic force that bursts out of him and creates a massive headway of realization.

What is new in the energy of the New Age? How is it manifested and how does it differ from the old energy?

The energy of the Age of Earth was connected to the **element of water** and **earth**, to a feeling of overload and lack of understanding. It was connected to the feeling that human beings were living a life of difficulty because they were controlled by emotion. The old energy created weakness and helplessness in human beings and caused them numerous rectifications.

In the old age, the connection to the **element of water** and the **element of earth** was necessary. The person at the end of the age did not know how to complete the emotional processes in his life. He was pulled into quagmires of negative emotions that were created from the **element of water**. These clouded his life with difficulty and frustration, but only from this place a person begins to search for answers for growth.

The meaning of energetic growth and spiritual development is to understand how to be rid of the difficulty of the **element of water** (emotion) and to connect to the **high element of air**, the **high element of fire** that drives a person to creation processes through light, to the **element of earth** that creates realization.

The combination of the four elements is necessary to balancing processes. Through them a person creates the inner burning within himself and does not allow any negative element to cause him to sink.

In the New Age, the **element of air** is the conductor, it pulls the strings of Creation and pulls the strings of the human soul. When the **element of air** pulls forward, the **element of fire**, through the inner burning, causes the **element of air** to move forward.

When there is no low emotion, there are no rectifications. Pettiness and quibbling between people do not exist. Speech and communication fill a proper role and create a real, correct, and direct communication. Only then does a person feel that the inner burning within him has become positive and creates in him the vision of the future and the vision of the goals, and these are the products of the **element of fire**. Thus, energy changes from thought-only processes.

A person must not sit idly by and create misunderstanding regarding processes that are taking place in his life. In the New Age people will live their lives through streaming and meaning, and the tempo of life and creation will have a great importance.

Anyone who does not know how to stream with the pace of life, of the New Age, will be left behind.

The New Age = Streaming, and anyone who does not know how to connect to streaming processes will find it difficult to connect to the energy of the New Age.

When a person is connected to insights and development, he is connected to the toolbox of new and balanced thinking as you have received in the above lessons. You need to understand that there is power in this information whose role it is to transform every person to become the leader and create meaning in his life.

We are not speaking of those who receive the connection naturally. We are speaking of those who want to enter the New Age, but are experiencing difficulty and fear lest their world be destroyed.

The world in the New Age will not be destroyed and will not break up. The world will enhance itself energetically and will accelerate in terms of insights and personal development.

You, as a human being, do not know what the future holds, just as you could not foresee your present in the past. But if you look at yourself ten years ago or five years ago, you will see that your life (particularly your technological life) have created openness, headways, understanding, and thought. When a person does not have to cope with emotion and difficulty in his life, he empowers himself and approaches a goal that is precise. Like a ballistic missile hitting a target.

When you connect to the energy of the New Age, you create growth that stems from internal cleansing, without the weight of emotion on your shoulders. When you feel clean and happy from within, you realize your life and connect to the energy of abundance.

Anyone who learns and develops spiritually, is enriching himself and his soul, and is opening the way to a highly powerful energy. This is the bonus you receive when you are in the process. You are preparing your vessel, your soul, and your body, for energy that will begin to apply its power in later stages. And as we said: You are the locomotive. You are the leader and you are the first, as opposed to the others who will wake up later.

EPILOGUE

- **In the last frequency, you have spoken of a headway. Do you have a message of headway for each of us?**

I **Elinos** stand before you, speaking through the voice of this one (Hayuta), creating your understanding essence.

At this moment, a door has opened on your path. I cannot decide for you whether you will cross the threshold or will remain in the same place.

I connect to this one (Hayuta) to create within her the tools for you. To you, who follow her path and create meaning on the path of your life, she gives the tools of insight through this information. It is up to you to understand and wish to take them and use these insights in your life.

When you asked to receive a blessing, blessings were given to you at each stage that you created an understanding.

The blessings emerged through the Creation energy into your bodies, down to the cellular level. Even if the words were unpleasant to your heart or your ears, or you thought that you were hearing those words as a broken record, you connected to the energy I created in you.

That is why I pass through her the knowledge and I give her the manner of speech, frequency and energy.

With your own hands, with your essence and especially with your will, you are meant to leap over the hedges of fear to pass the threshold towards your goal, mission and growth.

You need to know and understand that when tools are given to a person, he can put them aside, store them somewhere or use them.

Your job is to use the tools given to you. Take them and use them, create essence for insight and connection.

When I (**Elinus** - the name of the new energy) input my words into that one (Hayuta) and she passes them on to you, the process of hearing the frequency opens your ears to new insight, light and realization.

Your job is to accept, understand, and create growth processes through reading of knowledge. Each one has his own development, his own understanding and his own way.

Your existential life is in your hands. You create the reality of your life, and you create within you the meaningful way of understanding.

The connection to high intensities will begin when you apply what you now contain since we expect you to be the locomotive of your life, through which you will have numerous meanings.

And if you look at a train station crowded with people, you'll see people coming up and down the train and sometimes just passing, looking and not entering. But all the trains have many cars and only one locomotive.

You are the locomotive of many cars that are meant to accompany you through growth processes. Each in his own way, each in his own understandings and each in the meaning of his life. The choice is whether to operate the locomotive and lead your life on the significant train, or to leave the cars overnight (or throughout your life) for understanding. This is your choice alone. Our job is to create tools together with you.

We thank you and appreciate the one that creates insights from a meaningful perspective, since she has come as an emissary to create insights. Many people in Creation do not understand what the insights are, and it is her role to illuminate, through meaningful insights, and create breakthrough processes.

You need to know and understand that in your life you must grow your soul so that the locomotive of your life will be powerful and full of energy. Your mission also has the awareness of ascending people to an energetic level of understanding and insights, and to lead each person in his or her own way of life.

We thank you. Be blessed in your path, for you have chosen growth processes and light.

We, the guides, bless you and thank you.

> And I bless you and thank you for the privilege to read this blessed knowledge,
>
> And I am grateful to everyone who accompanied me on my spiritual path,
>
> My family, my students, and my patients
>
> And to you my dear guides, thank you from the bottom of my heart for having you in my life, to accompany me in my important and special way.
>
> Thank you very much.
> **Hayuta**

Made in the USA
Columbia, SC
23 April 2021